*"Truth can never be told
so as to be understood
and not be believed."*

WILLIAM BLAKE

Islam
Reviewed

by
M. Ali

2<small>ND</small> AMERICAN EDITION

FISH HOUSE PUBLISHING

Copyright 1999

NOTE

Except otherwise indicated
Bible passages are taken from
the King James Version.

Koranic references are based on the Text,
Translation and Commentary by A. Yusuf Ali.

The author, M. Ali, is a former Muslim
whom the Lord graciously saved in 1985.
Since then God put a burden in his heart
to evangelize Muslims.
He does this by direct preaching,
writing specialized tracts, books and literature,
mobilizing Christians for the great commission
and conducting teaching seminars
on how to reach Muslims for Christ.
He may be contacted through
the publisher.

ISBN 0-9628139-7-4

FISH HOUSE PUBLISHING
P. O. Box 453, Fort Myers, FL 33902, USA

Printed in the United States of America

Publisher's Note

Church-goers in America have no idea of what it is like to stand for Jesus in the face of severe persecution. Christians in mortal danger live so far away that their trials aren't real to us. But if you were there, ah, then the inhuman oppression of it all would hit you in the face like a hammer blow. You would discover that speaking out for Jesus could be suicidal. Many of your friends would be in hiding, in jail, or lying face down in some muddy ditch – just a few more infidel corpses rotting unmourned in the tropical sun.

In the Sudan, Christians by the hundreds of thousands have been slaughtered, many by crucifixion. In Nigeria, many thousands more have been killed. One African brother (attending a Bible College here in the United States) plans to return home to begin a Christian school in his native land, but he knows he will not last more than a year or two before they kill him.

So what kind of people would act with such cruel hatred toward defenseless men and women who wished them no harm? The radical Muslims, that's who, in an Islamic Jihad or so-called "holy war" they have been waging against Christians and Jews for over 1300 years.

M. Ali (*not his real name*) has seen some of the above with his own eyes, so he writes about Islam from personal experience. Ali is a well-educated former Muslim who came to the Lord and is now a minister of the Gospel. Because of his background, Ali is particularly well suited to compare the Bible to the Koran and history, and he does so in such a way that truths about which he writes literally jump off the page at you.

We may not be able to relate to every word this dear brother has written. But that shouldn't matter to us for a minute. What counts is that Ali is a stalwart brother in a foreign land who, at the risk of his life, is standing for Jesus against a murderous enemy. And wonder of it all, though they have killed his Christian friends and burned their churches, Ali still sees Muslims as precious souls for whom Jesus died. As a result, he is an example to us all on how to love and witness to Muslims in the face of their virulent animosity.

Contents

Introduction

Islam is one of the world's fastest growing religions. About one billion people are said to profess faith in it. Besides its numerical growth, Islam also seems to be the only religion in the universe that openly challenges Christianity.

Islam opposes the cardinal teachings of Christianity such as the sonship of Christ, the fatherhood of God and the death of Jesus Christ. Because of these opposing doctrinal views, the need to review Islam is critical to those who hunger for truth. The teachings on the person of Christ determine the genuineness or falsity of any religion. Without Christ, all religions could be right. So from the outset, we are going to be reviewing Islam, based on its teachings on Christ and other Biblical doctrines. We must face the issues raised in this book squarely as they have eternal consequences for our souls, be we Christian or Muslim.

Therefore, I adjure you, in the name of the Lord, to be open-hearted and patient as you journey with me through the pages of this book. This book wasn't written for argument sake (we have had plenty of that in the past without positive results), but rather to challenge you to eternal life. If you are one of those who has closed his heart to the truth, then this book will be of little or no help to you (You need special prayer for deliverance). I strongly believe that polemical somersaults, however logical they may seem, will avail nothing before the judgement throne of God on the last day.

Truth can sometimes be exceedingly hot and bitter. If you find any statement in this book to be offensive, be sure it is not intended to be. For courtesy sake, throughout this book I use the Koranic translation accepted by all Muslims (Yusuf Ali's) and the recognized Hadiths.

Since it takes humility, open-mindedness and prayer to understand the things of God, I advise you to pray genuinely – in whatever language – that God should reveal to you the truth in this book, or the lies (if any), and you can be certain of His help, if you pray to Him sincerely.

Chapter 1

Islam & the Sonship of Christ

Attributing fatherhood to God is condemned vehemently by Allah in the Koran. In fact, it is regarded as blasphemy. This is one of the reasons that Muslims believe the Bible texts have been corrupted. They are of the opinion that Jesus never addressed Himself with any title of Sonship.[1] This title is so repulsive to Allah that he even resorted to outright cursing in one of the suras in the Koran:

> "...The Christians call Christ the Son of God. That is a saying from their mouth. [*In this*] they but imitate what the unbelievers of old used to say. God's curse be upon them.." (Surat at-taubah, 30).

If Allah is really the Rahman Rahim (i.e. the Beneficent, the Merciful) why doesn't he wish that the "blasphemous" Christians repent? Why resort to outright cursing? Yet in the Bible, God has to bear with even Satan until the appointed time. Why can't Allah bear with Christians? At this point, one is forced to ask: who is this Allah that has to resort to cursing those who believe that Jesus is the Son of God? Could he be the same God that spoke in the Bible? If the Bible and the Koran had the same author, would they not definitely speak the same thing?

---

[1] Historic Note: In Jerusalem, on the ancient temple mount of God most Holy, Abd al-Malik ibn Marwan, in 688 AD, built the Dome of the Rock as a memorial to Muhammad. The Dome was erected just 300 feet south of where the Solomonic Temple once stood, and only a few hundred yards from where Jesus was crucified. Within the Dome is a prominent inscription in Arabic that reads: "God forbid that He should have a Son."

Chapter 2

The Bible & the Sonship of Christ

Let us consider the testimony of Angel Gabriel.

> "Then said Mary unto the Angel [*Gabriel*] how shall this be, seeing I know not a man? And the angel answered and said unto her, the Holy Ghost shall overshadow thee, therefore also that Holy Thing which shall be born of thee shall be called the Son of God" (Luke 1:34-35).

When Jesus was baptized in the River Jordan, the Gospel says:

> "And lo a voice from heaven, saying, this is my beloved Son in whom I am well pleased" (Matthew 3:17).

On yet another occasion, while on the mountain of transfiguration the Bible has the following to say:

> "And after six days Jesus taketh Peter, James and John his brother and bringeth them up into a high mountain apart, And was transfigured before them, and his face did shine as the sun, and His raiment was white as the light. And behold, there appeared unto them Moses and Elias talking with Him. Then answered Peter and said unto Jesus, Lord, it is good for us to be here. If thou wilt, let us make here three tabernacles; one for thee, and one for Moses, and one for Elias. While he yet spake, behold a bright cloud over-shadowed them and behold a voice out of the cloud, which said: This is my beloved Son in whom I am well pleased, hear ye him" (Matthew 17:1-5).

Writing later, one of the eye witnesses (Peter) testifies thus:

> "For we have not followed cunningly devised fables, when we made known unto you the power and coming of our Lord Jesus Christ but were eye witnesses of His Majesty. For He received from God the Father, honour and glory when there came a voice to Him from the excellent glory, this is my beloved Son, in whom

I am well pleased. And this voice which came from heaven we heard, when we were with Him in the holy mount" (2 Peter 1:16-18).

Anyone who has the slightest knowledge about the nature of God would admit that the ever-consistent God, the true God, the God of Abraham, Isaac and Jacob would never have sent any "angel Gabriel" about 600 years later to refute this Bible teaching. Only hearts that have been influenced by the jinns (demons) would believe otherwise. Those who have been misled into believing that Christians and Muslims worship the same God need to review their position. In the Bible, God acknowledges Jesus as His Son on many occasions, while in the Koran, Allah vigorously rejects it. The truth is that only Satan can teach in opposition to God's word. That Satan can assign one of his angels to pose as an "angel Gabriel" is clear from the following passage of scripture:

"And no marvel, for Satan himself is transformed into an angel of light. Therefore it is no great a thing if his ministers also be transformed as the ministers of righteousness: whose end shall be according to their works" (2 Corinthians 11:14-15).

If one really ponders the Koranic verses that object to the Sonship of Christ, he is forced to query the ignorance of whoever is speaking. Sura 6, Al-An'am, 101 says:

"To Him is due the primal origin of the heavens and the earth: how can he have a son when he hath no consort [*wife*]?[1] He created all things and he hath full knowledge of all things."

Can you imagine God to be so carnal as to ask a question any Sunday School child would not ask? (Whoever composed this ayat failed to start with Lo! or Say, so as to create the impression that an Allah was speaking). Could Allah be so shallow of knowledge as not to know of any

---

[1] Muslims believe that Christians, in calling Christ the Son of God, are guilty of making a man into God (a blasphemy), and that Christians also believe that God married and biologically produced a child. Allah knew better, this ayat teaches an untruth that has deceived Muslims throughout time and kept them from coming to the only One who could save them from their sins. Christ did not become the Son of God by reason of the virgin birth, but through the virgin birth a part of God's Being became man. Christians did not take a man and make him God; they worship God who came to earth in the form of a man. (John 1:1, 14).

sonship other that a biological sonship? Doesn't whoever is speaking in this sura know of legal sonship, Adoption? Doesn't he know of metaphorical sonships e.g., an Egyptian as son of the Nile, Arab as son of the desert, necessity as the mother of invention, a student as the son of knowledge, etc.? When the Bible teaches that Christ is the Son of God, it does not mean God married a wife and begat Jesus in the usual biological process, as the Koranic Allah declares. *Jesus is the unique Son of God in a spiritual sense.* Because of the marvelous love the Bible God has towards sinners, He came down to us in the person of Jesus Christ. He became known to us as God's Son and He came to save us from our sins.

> "And without controversy, great is the mystery of godliness: God was manifest in the flesh, justified in the Spirit, seen of angels, preached unto the Gentiles, believed on in the world, received up into glory" (1 Timothy 3:16).

Muslims cannot imagine God loving sinners to the extent of coming down personally, as the Son, to save them. To Muslims this is evidence of polytheism, because they are taught in the Koran that Allah does not love sinners (Sura 2:190). This is repeated twenty four times in the Koran for emphasis. That Allah does not love unbelievers (Sura 3:31) and that he has even blocked their ears, sealed their hearts and blindfolded their eyes (Sura 2:6-7). All these are in direct opposition to Bible teachings which instruct that:

> "God commended His love towards us, in that, while we were yet sinners Christ died for us" (Roman 5:8).

The central theme of the Bible is this:

> "For God so loved the world that he gave His only begotten Son that whosoever believeth in Him should not perish but have everlasting life" (John 3:16)

Are you a sinner? You know down in your heart that you are. You also know in your heart that without the shedding of blood there is no forgiveness. But in spite of all your sins, the Bible God loves you and has made provision for your salvation through His perfect sacrifice, the shed blood of Jesus, His only Son.

Chapter 3

The Cross
in Islam

The death and resurrection of Jesus is another issue that arouses controversy in Islam. The Bible plainly teaches that God, in love, offered up Jesus on the cross of Calvary for our sins and raised Him again the third day for our justification. But the Koran says half "No" and half "Yes," thereby leaving Muslims confused. In an attempt to justify the ambiguous teaching of the Koran on the issue, some Islamic scholars allege corruption of the Bible. Half "Yes" and half "No," in the sense that they are divided over the interpretation of Surat al-Imran, 55:

> "Behold! God said: O Jesus! I will take thee to Myself and clear thee [*of the falsehoods*] of those who blaspheme; I will make those who follow thee superior to those who reject faith, to the day of resurrection: then shall ye all return to me and I will judge between you of the matters wherein ye dispute."

The word Arabic "inni-mutawaffeeka" translated "I will take thee" is the point of controversy among scholars. Some hold that the word means death of sleep and God raised him in his sleep.[1] Others say the word means I, God, "take you" from the world, but not by death.[2] Yet others claim it means God caused Jesus to die three hours and then raised him.[3] Muhammad Ibn Ishaq said, he was dead seven hours, then God raised him to life and took him to heaven. Dr. Anis Shorrosh says:[4] "As an Arab, I have never known of any other meaning than death for this expression, i.e. 'inni-mutawaffeeka', within or outside the Koran." Sura 4, An-nisa, 157 which follows, does nothing to clear up these muddy waters:

---

[1] Al-Muthana says he was told so by Ishaq who in turn heard it from Abd-Allah Ibn Jafar and Al-Rabia

[2] Ali Ibn Suhail from Domra Ibn Rabia from Ibn Shuthab from Matar Waraq

[3] Ibn Hamid quoting Salima and Ibn Ishaq and Wahab Ibn Munabih

[4] *Islam Revealed: A Christian Arab View of Islam*, p. 97

"That they said [*in boast*], 'We killed Christ Jesus the son of Mary, the Apostle of God;' But they killed him not, nor crucified him, but so it was made to appear to them, and those who differ therein are full of doubts, with no [*certain*] knowledge, but only conjecture to follow, for of a surety they killed him not."

From the above sura came the Muslim theory that Allah must have cast the likeness of Jesus onto another man – and that Jesus was snatched up into heaven while the other man was crucified. According to Muslims, the world has been deceived into believing that Jesus was crucified. But the chief culprit in this deception is Allah himself. Whoever invented this clever fable actually did a fairly good job for Islam, but not a thorough one. He forgot to identify this so-called Jesus substitute, thereby creating more doctrinal controversies.

Muslims deem it convenient to select Judas Iscariot since he was the one that betrayed Jesus. But that cannot be correct. Judas was overwhelmed with guilt after the betrayal of his Master and he committed suicide (Matthew 27:3-5). So Muslims must swim and eventually sink in this ocean-wide doctrinal dilemma into which Allah and Koran have immersed them (unless they repent).

Realizing the untenable nature of the ambiguous statement in Sura 4:157, some Islamic scholars are proposing other more "enlightened" theories. One such pundit is the aggressive sophist, Ahmed Deedat. In one of his specious arguments entitled *Resurrection or Resuscitation?*, Deedat proposes the "swoon theory" – a dubious conjecture at best – that Jesus survived the cross half dead and recovered afterwards in a roomy grave.[1]

The repeated denial of Jesus' death on the cross in Sura 4:157 not only exposes Allah's deception, but it also exposes his ignorance of prophetic tradition. The true God mentioned the triumph of Messiah (Jesus) over Satan through death when He gave the promise in the garden of Eden (Genesis 3:15). The Prophet Isaiah predicted His (Jesus) virgin birth (Isaiah 7:14) and also His atoning death (Isaiah 53:5-9). The

---

[1] This theory was first conceived by Venturni, a German rationalist and then popularized by Prophet Ahman Ghulam of the Ahmadiya brand of Islam. Deedat implies, had he lived in Muhammad's time and been in the shoes of either Zaid Ibn Thabit or Waraqa Ibn Naufal, that he would have suggested this seemingly "sophisticated" swoon concept himself. Deedat is about 1,400 years too late for his warmed over theory to be seriously considered.

Prophet David, whom Muslims call Anabiya Dauda, also prophesied Jesus' death (Psalm 16:10), a prophecy which is confirmed in Acts 13:32-35.

If you are the kind of person who is skeptical of fulfilled prophecies, then consider one that will be fulfilled at Christ's second coming:

> "And I will pour upon the house of David and upon the inhabitants of Jerusalem, the Spirit of Grace and supplications; and they shall look upon me whom they have pierced". (Zech 12:10; CF. Rev. 1:7).

An Allah who is ignorant of these prophecies cannot be a true God even if he claims to be one. As we see in Surat al-Maryam, 15:

> "So peace on him [*refers to John*] the day he was born, the day that he dies and the day that he will be raised up alive [*again*]!"

And verse 33 of the same sura:

> "So peace is on me [*Jesus*] the day I was born, the day that I die, and the day I shall be raised up to life."

There is no arguing the fact that Muslims believe the Apostle John (Yahaya) was born and died according to the first verse. Then why not believe the same of Jesus the Christ according to the second verse? Because the order of the two verses is the same and the wordings are practically the same. The context in the second can only mean one thing. Yusuf Ali seems to realize this fact. [1] In comparing Sura 19:15 with Sura 19:33, he commented thus:

> "Christ was not crucified (Sura 4:157) but those who believed He never died should ponder over this verse (i.e. 33 of Surat al-Maryam)".

Some do not want to believe the crucifixion on the ground that God would not have allowed His chosen prophet like Jesus to be killed by wicked hands. Such reasoning is refuted by the Koran itself.

They (also) said:

> "God took our promise not to believe in an apostle unless he showed us a sacrifice consumed by fire [*from heaven*]. Say: 'there came to you apostles before me, with clear signs and even with

---

[1] No. 2485, Ali, A. Yusuf, *The Quran: Text, Translation and Commentary*

what ye ask for: why then did ye slay them, if ye speak the truth?'" (Sura 3:183).

If we examine the whole Koran, we find that the only messenger who came from God with the kind of offering described in the above quoted sura is Christ as can be seen in Sura 5:115-117.

The Apostle Paul, whom Muslims hate to hear, made an amazing remark concerning the death and resurrection of Jesus Christ. A remark which makes a mockery of anyone trying to deny this historical event.

"For I delivered unto you first of all that which I also received, how that Christ died for our sins according to the scriptures; And that He was buried, and that He arose again the third day according to the Scriptures: And that He was seen of Cephas, then of the twelve: After that, He was seen of above five hundred brethren at once; of whom the greater part remain unto this present, but some are fallen asleep" (1 Corinthians 15:3-6).

In essence, the Apostle Paul is saying this: if you are in doubt, go and ask the eyewitnesses. If the Muslims knew the importance of the cross in God's program, they certainly would not have rejected it. Satan knows that he met his Waterloo through the death and resurrection of Jesus:

"Forasmuch then as the children are partakers of flesh and blood, he also Himself [*Jesus*] likewise took part of the same; that through death he might destroy him that hath the power of death, that is the devil; And deliver them who through fear of death were all their life time subject to bondage" (Hebrews 2:14, 15).

This was the sole mission of Christ and He accomplished it, praise God. Contrary to Muslim allegations, neither Christ nor Paul established a religion. Religion is Satan's dragnet to catch men into Hell-fire, while Christ came purposely to conquer Satan and deliver as many as put their trust in Him. Does the Koran inform us of how Allah defeated Satan? No, on the contrary, Allah even incorporates Satan's cohorts (the jinns – demons) into the Islamic fold (Sura 72:14), and concentrates on fighting against the Salvation plan of the Bible God.

Dear reader, do not allow the enemy to rob you of the Salvation made available through the atoning death and triumphant resurrection of Jesus. As a result of your sins, you owe God a debt you can never pay. His perfect holiness demands justice, a justice which would result in a punishment for every offence. But He is also a God of love. In His love He yearns to be merciful. But if He merely waved our sins aside (as some think), the yearning of His love would be met, but what about the requirement of His holiness and justice? My friend, there must be a basis for forgiveness. The cross provides that basis. Jesus Christ died to pay your sin debt. The Bible God knew – if He left mankind alone – that everyone would go to Hell, for no one can satisfy the demands of God's righteousness. That was why God, in love, came in the person of Jesus. He came to help us.

"But God commendeth his love toward us, in that, while we were yet sinners, Christ died for us" (Romans 5:7)

Chapter 4

Textual History of the Koran

Almost every Muslim is taught from infancy to cling to the notion that the Bible has been corrupted and changed, while the Koran is free from corruption, perfectly preserved since the time of Muhammad. But a thorough study of the textual history of the Koran will show that it is not the Bible, but the Koran that has been changed. That is what Islamic historians themselves bequeathed to us.

After the famous battle of Aqraba in 632 AD, during the Caliphate of Abu Bakr, many Muslims who knew the Koran by heart were killed. As a result, Umar B. Al-Khattab advised Abu Bakr of the need to compile the Koran into a standardized text. Abu Bakr ordered the compilation to be made by Zaid Ibn Thabit from inscriptions on palm leaves, stones and from the remaining reciters.

When the compilation was done, it was kept by Abu Bakr until his death. His successor, Umar, then took custody of it. Afterward, it came into the possession of Hafsa, one of Muhammad's widows (a daughter of Umar).[1] The companions of the prophet also did their own compilations and produced other manuscripts for use in various provinces. There were four rival provinces, each using a different text of the Koran.[2]

During the reign of Khalif Uthman (the third Khalifah), reports reached him that in various parts of Syria, Armenia and Iraq, Muslims were reciting the Koran differently from the way it was being recited by Arabian Muslims. Uthman immediately sent for the manuscript in Hafsa's possession and ordered Zaid Ibn Thabit and three others, Abdullah Ibn

---

[1] See *Mishkatul Massabih*, ch. 3

[2] In Kufa, the manuscript of Abdullah ibn Masud was in use. That of Ubyy Ibn Ka'b was in the possession of the Syrians. The one edited by Migdad Ibn Amr was in circulation in the province of Hims. While that of Abu Musa al-Ash'ari was in use in Basra, Iraq.

Zubair, Said Ibn Al-As and Abdullah Al-Rahman Ibn Harith B. Hisham to make copies of the text and make corrections where necessary. When these were completed, we read that Uthman took violent action regarding other existing Koranic manuscripts:

> "Uthman sent to every Muslim province one copy of what they had copied and ordered that all the other koranic materials, whether written in fragmentary manuscripts, whole copies, to be burnt." (Sahih al-Bukhari Vol. 6 Page 479).

To eliminate variant readings and contradictions, all other manuscripts were indeed burned, but the Uthmanic edition itself was not perfect and met with a similar fate. When Marwan was governor of Medina, he ordered Hafsa's manuscript to be destroyed. The only reasonable conclusion one can have is that during Uthman's time some of the contradictions in Hafsa's text were so glaring that a total destruction of it was called for rather than revision. From then until now, conflicting passages and historical inaccuracies exist within the Koranic texts.

The Deedats, the Joommals, and the so-called Sheiks continue their unwarranted attack on the Bible while suppressing the fact that Khalif Uthman burned all the Koranic manuscripts apart from Hafsa's, and that Governor Marwan followed the example of Uthman by destroying the Hafsa text as well. Anyone with the slightest regard for truth would have to admit that the *Textus Receptus* of the Koran now in circulation is a far cry from the *textus originalis*! It is not too wild to suggest that were Muhammad alive at the time of these incidents, he would have received one of his usual "revelations" to back up those burnings.

Contrary to Muslim belief, there were more than just language differences between Uthman's text and the texts which were ordered to be burned. In every case, there were considerable verbal differences between them and the text Uthman determined (by whim) to be the final standardized version of the Koran.

These differences were real textual variants and not just language peculiarities as is often taken for granted. In several cases there were words and sentences found in some codices that were missing in others. In other instances, the variants concerned whole clauses and consonantal variants in certain words. No wonder Khalif Uthman had to resort to wholesale burning as his best option.[1]

Evidence abounds to this day, that verses, indeed whole passages are missing from the Koran that is in circulation today. For instance, the second Khalifah, Khalif Umar, stated in his life-time that certain verses prescribing stoning for adultery were recited by Prophet Muhammad himself as part of the Koran:

> "God sent Muhammad and sent down the scripture to him. Part of what he sent down was the passage on stoning. We read it, we were taught it, and we heeded it. The apostle stoned and we stoned after him. I fear that in time to come men will say that they find no mention of stoning in God's book and thereby go astray in neglecting an ordinance which God has sent down. Verily, stoning in the book of God is a penalty laid on married men and women who commit adultery." (Ibn Ishaq, Sirat Rasulullah p. 684)

The verse on stoning, no longer to be found in the Koran, is incontrovertible proof that the Koran as it stands today is not the same as the one spoken by Muhammad.

What the public does not know is that Jihad has many faces. Jihad is not just slaughtering people for Islam, but it is also a systematic suppression of truth and propagation of lies.[2] If not, how can Muslims boldly assert (despite hard historic evidence to the contrary) that the

---

[1] See Jeffery, *Materials for the History of the Text of the Koran*, pp. 24-114. The author has gone to considerable effort to collect solid evidence from the many Islamic sources that are documented in this book.

[2] Archeological Note: In support of M. Ali's statement: the true site of Mt. Sinai was found over two decades ago by the archeologist Ron Wyatt. Sinai is now known to be Jebel el-Lawz on the Arabian Peninsula. It is right where the Bible has been saying it was all along (see Galatians 4:25). However, the Saudi government has surrounded the Mt. Sinai site with a chain-link fence and suppressed the information, probably because of the devastating effect that discovery could have on the validity of Islam and the Koran. If the information on that site were to be released, it would discredit the Islamic claim that the Bible has been corrupted. That site, the artifacts thereon (and similar sites in Arabia such as Rephidim), exactly fit the Bible's description of the Israelite wilderness wanderings. Those sites prove the Bible to be both accurate and true. (Videos of that ancient site and many others are available from Wyatt Archeological Research, 713 Lambert Dr., Nashville, TN 37220).

Bible has been changed while the Koran has been perfectly preserved since Muhammad's time?

You cannot tell me that Islamic scholars are ignorant of the many defects in the Koran, nor of the havoc that the various Khalifs have done to it.[1] We, ourselves, are not in any way amazed for the Bible has said:

> "Such teachings [*Propaganda*] come through hypocritical liars, whose consciences have been seared as with a hot iron"
> (1 Timothy 4:2, NIV)

The plain truth is that the Koran has been changed through suppression and burning, and many of its passages have been deliberately removed or altered.

---

[1] At least, M.O.A. Abdul, in his book entitled *Studies in Islamic Series,* vol. 3, pp. 19-20, 1st printing 1971, mentioned the incidents that led Khalif Uthman to burn Koranic manuscripts.

Koran &
the Bible
on Historic Facts

As is characteristic of him, the Islamic scholar, A. Deedat, always attempts to discredit the Bible. On p. 6 of his little booklet titled *Christ in Islam,* he labors to prove that Jesus' right name was Esau in Hebrew, Eesa or Isa in Arabic. We know where he and his likes are headed with that idea. They just want to justify an error in the Koran. The name Jesus is the anglicized form of Jehoshua, meaning Jehovah is Savior.[1] The name was given by God Himself through the Angel Gabriel as recorded in Luke Chapter one, verse Thirty-one:

> "And behold, thou shalt conceive in thy womb, and bring forth a Son, and shall call his name JESUS."

Esau was the twin brother of Jacob, who sold his birthright to Jacob for a bowl of porridge (Genesis 25: 32-34). When Esau missed the blessing as a result of his folly, he became angry and started persecuting Jacob (Genesis 27:41). The nation of Israel descended from Jacob. The other name of Esau is Edom (red) and the Edomite nation descended from him. Possibly because of the bitter hatred of Esau towards his brother Israel (Jacob), Israelites do not name their children Esau to this day. Muhammad, or whoever composed the Koran, must have been misled by his informants. Jesus, not Isa, is the proper name of the miracle man that descended from heaven and made His landing on Nazareth soil

---

[1] The word in the original is *Iησοῦς* (Strong's Greek Lexicon No. G2424). i.e., Iesous, (ee-ay-sooce), which is the Greek form of the Hebrew name Jehoshua. (Strong's Hebrew Lexicon No. 3091). The meaning of which is "Jehovah saves" or "Jehovah saved." Pronounced in Hebrew: Yeh-ho-shoo'-ah; from H3068 and H3467; Jehoshua (i.e. Joshua), Comp. H1954, H3442.

(1 Corinthians 15:47, Acts 10:38). Even Arabian Christians use the Arabic equivalent, Yesu, for Jesus.

The Koran confused Miriam, sister of Aaron, with Mary mother of Jesus. Here is the confused passage as stated in Surat Maryam, 27-29:

> "At length she brought the [babe] to her people, carrying him [in her arms]. They said: 'O Mary! truly an amazing thing hast thou brought! O Sister of Aaron! thy father was not a man of evil, nor thy mother a woman unchaste!' But she pointed to the babe. They said: 'how can we talk to one who is a child in the cradle?'"

According to Islam, Amran (Imran) was the father of the Virgin Mary (also Sura 3:30-44). Any child who attended a Sunday School knows that Miriam, sister of Aaron and Moses lived 1,400 years before Mary the mother of Jesus. (see Exodus 15:20 and Numbers 26:30-44).

Islamic scholars seem to have detected this error, but instead of rectifying it, they hide it in interpretive argument, claiming that the sister of or brother of Aaron means a descendant of, or of the clan of Aaron.[1] Aaron, elder brother of Moses, son of Amran (Imram) was a priest of Levitical descent (Exodus 4:14; Numbers 26:59). While the Virgin Mary, Mother of Jesus, was of the tribe of Judah, and of the lineage of David (Psalm 132:11; Luke 1:32; Romans 1:3).

> "For it is clear that our Lord [Jesus] descended from Judah, and in regard to that tribe Moses said nothing about priests" (Hebrews 7:14 NIV).

It is evident that Miriam, sister of Aaron, and the Virgin Mary were neither blood nor tribal relatives, nor were they of the same descent. Miriam descended from Levi, while Mary descended from Judah. These were two distinct tribes and lineages in Israel. The Muslims' belief in the infallibility of the Koran (without verification) obliges them to pitch their tent with the Koran even if it teaches that 1+1=3. As past actions and rhetoric show, Islamic scholars will try to justify the Koranic position no matter how historically untenable their positions may be.

---

[1] See pamphlet entitled *Jesus in the Qur'an and the Bible*, an outline, by Jamal Badawi, p. 1; cf. Yusuf Ali's commentary No. 2481.

The name of Abraham's father was not Azar, as the Koran states in Sura 6:74, but Terah (Genesis 11:26). The Koran further teaches that Pharaoh's wife adopted Moses (Sura 28:8,9), whereas Moses himself said he was adopted by Pharaoh's daughter (Exodus 2:5-10).

In several places the Koran associates Haman with a Pharaoh of Moses' time (Sura 28:6-7, 38; 40:24, 36), but from the Bible book of Esther (3:1-10), we know that Haman was a servant of Ahasuerus I, the 5th century BC Medo-Persian king (known to us all as Xerxes) who lost the battle of Marathon. So Haman was really born a thousand years after Moses!

In the words of Sura 28:28 and 40:36,37, Pharaoh commanded Haman to build a tower of bricks, the top of which will reach heaven. We know from archaeological and other historic evidence that this famous tower was built in the Babylonian plain many generations before Pharaoh's time (Genesis 11:1-9). The account of Gideon, son of Joash who led the Israelites in battle against the Midianites is given in Judges Chapter 7, but in relating this incident the Koran makes another error, stating that this took place at the time of Saul in connection with David's victory over Goliath (Sura 2:249-251).

Chapter 6

Islam
& Fables

The Bible book of Genesis records the murder of Abel by his brother Cain. There is also an account of this event in the Koran (Sura 5:30-35). However, at the concluding part of the Koranic story, we find an unusual assertion which has no parallel in the Bible record:

"Then God sent a raven, who scratched the ground, to show him how to hide the shame [*corpse*] of his brother" (Sura 5:34)

If that assertion is true, then one should marvel at how a holy God could not only wink at a cold-blooded murder, but also support the murderer by helping Cain to hide the body.

Well, according to Muslims, Islam did not start with Muhammad. By their doctrine, Cain could have been a Muslim, and the murder of his brother could have been an act of Jihad. If we accept that line of reasoning, we can then understand how Allah justifies what the Bible God condemns (Genesis 4:10). The point is this: Sura 5:34 quoted above is similar to stories in a Jewish book of fables, where it is recorded that Adam wept for Abel and did not know what to do with his corpse until he saw a raven scratch the ground and bury its dead companion (Pirke Rabbi Eliezer, chapter 21).

In the Koran, it is Cain who saw the raven and in the Jewish book of fables, it is Adam. Apart from that slight difference; the weird similarity between the two narratives cannot be overlooked. Since the Jewish book predates the Koran, it appears that Muhammad (with the aid of his secretaries) plagiarized the story and made a convenient adjustment that would fit his divine "revelation." This conclusion is reinforced when we consider the very next verse in the Koran:

"On that account: we ordained for the children of Israel that if any man slew a person – unless it be for murder or for spreading mischief in the land – it would be as if he slew the whole people and if anyone saved a life, it would be as if he saved the life of the whole people" (Sura 5:35)

At first glance, this verse seems to have no link with the preceding story. Why the life or death of one should be as the salvation or destruction of all mankind is unclear. But when we turn to another Jewish book of folklore we find a similar tale. We read the following in the Mishnah translated by H. Danby:

"We find it is said in the case of Cain who murdered his brother: 'The voice of thy brother's blood crieth' (Genesis 4:10). It is not said here blood in the singular but blood in the plural, that is, his own blood and the blood of his seed. Man was created single in order to show that to him who kills a single individual it shall be reckoned that he has slain that whole race, but to him who preserves the life of a single individual, it is counted that he hath preserved the whole race." (Mishnah Sanhedrin 4:5).

In the reasoning of the Jewish rabbi who wrote these words, the use of the plural blood in the Bible indicates not only the blood of one man but that of his whole progeny. Whether the Rabbi's speculative interpretation is right or not, is not the issue. The issue is this: why should a Koran that is alleged to have been revealed by Allah contain a corrupted restatement of an existing rabbinical interpretation of a Biblical passage?

The Koranic story of Abraham is patterned after the Biblical account, but when it digresses, the departure can usually be traced to Jewish fables. For instance, the Koran narrates a story about Abraham's father and his idolatrous community. According to the Koran, Abraham (the monotheist) is alleged to have destroyed all the idols except the chief one. When questioned as to who broke the idols, he mockingly told them to inquire from the spared idol as to what happened to the rest. This made the mob angry and they supposedly threw Abraham into burning fire, but Allah made the fire cool and rescued him from their evil plot. This story is recorded in Sura 21, Al-Anbiya, 51-70. As expected, that is a story with striking similarities to one recorded in Jewish folklore.

Incidentally, this fable was built around a mistranslation of a Hebrew word in Genesis 15:7. A Jewish scribe by the name Jonathan Ben Uzziel mistook "Ur" for "Or" (meaning fire), and rendered the verse "I am the

Lord who brought you out of the fire of the Chaldeans." The Koranic fable was welded around that palpable error.[1] What God did say in Genesis 15:7 was:

"I am the Lord that brought thee out of Ur of the Chaldees"

A brief quotation of the Jewish version in the "Midrash Rabah" will prove its striking similarity to the Koranic narrative which is widely alleged to be a revelation from Allah.

"Abraham broke all the idols with one axe except the biggest one and then placed the axe in the hand of the idol he spared. Now his father heard the commotion and ran to investigate and saw Abraham leaving as he arrived. When he was accused by his father, he said he gave them meat to eat but the others went for the food without waiting for the biggest to do so first, so the biggest one took the axe and shattered them all! Then his father enraged by Abraham's reply went to Nimrod who threw Abraham into fire but God then stepped in and save him from it."

The similarity between those two narratives is inescapable. That a story from Jewish folklore found its way into the Koran as historic reality should cause any thoughtful Muslim to doubt the alleged inspiration of the Koran. The Koran's penchant for fables reaches its climax in Surat an - Namil, 18:

"At length, when they came to a [*lowly*] valley of ants, one of the ants said: "O ye ants, get into your habitations, lest Solomon and his hosts crush you [*under foot*] without knowing it" (27:18).

If you explain the verse away as a metaphor, then you are wrong, for Solomon is alleged to have smiled at the speech of the ant (Verse 19). Who says Koran is not an "ultimate miracle"? An ant commanding and talking, indeed!

---

[1] Ur was a place that archaeological evidence shows to have existed during the time of Abraham. Ur is also mentioned elsewhere in Scripture (Genesis 11:31). The location is believed to be in Southern Iraq, by the River Euphrates, at the present day site of Tel-el-Muqayyar.

Chapter 7

Contradictions in the Koran

Contrary to the Muslim claim that the Koran is perfect and free from contradiction, the Koran is not only a bundle of contradictions, but a volume of confusion. The following examples prove the point:

> "Those who believe [*in the Qur'an*], and those who follow the Jewish [*Scriptures*], and the Christians and the Sabians, any one who believe in God and the last day, and work righteousness shall have their reward with their Lord: on them shall be no fear, nor shall they grieve." (Sura 2:62).

Now, read a counter "revelation" in Sura Imran:

> "If anyone desires a religion other than Islam [*Submission to God*] he will be in the ranks of those who have lost all spiritual good" (Sura 3:85)

The Koran rightly condemns hypocrisy (Sura 4:138; 9:64-68) and teaches that hypocrites will occupy the lowest part of Hell fire, (Sura 4:145). Yet Allah commands Muhammad to compel men to Islam at the point of the sword, i.e., in a Jihad (see Sura 47:4; 2:191; 4:74-77) while elsewhere stating that there should be no compulsion in religion (Sura 2:256). These statements cannot be logically reconciled. To condemn religious coercion while making Jihad incumbent on Muslims is surely hypocritical and an obvious contradiction.

In Sura 2:6-7, Muhammad is told that his attempt to convert the unbelievers will not avail anything because Allah has sealed their heart and their ears and blindfolded their eyes. But elsewhere Muhammad is told to attempt their conversion, by peaceful means anyway (Sura

24:54). In Surat al-Ghashiya, Muhammad is reminded of his role as a warner only and that the disbelievers will be punished by Allah himself.

'Thou art not one to manage [*men's*] affairs. But if any turn away and reject God, God will punish him with a mighty punishment, for to us will be their return." (Sura 88:22-25).

The very contrary is taught in other passages as the great prophet of Islam claims that Allah has commanded him to spread Islam with the sword. In Sura 4:48, 116, we learned that Shirk,[1] (idolatry) is an unpardonable sin, yet Abraham (Ibrahim), the friend of God, is alleged to be guilty of this sin (see Sura 6:75-78).

The power to create and impart life is the exclusive right of God alone. He cannot permit angels or prophets to create life or they would also be God. Yet Koran on the one hand teaches that Jesus fashioned a bird out of clay and imparted life into the bird (Sura 3:49), while on the other hand, the same Koran teaches that Jesus is no more than a prophet.

It is common knowledge that only God is worthy of worship, yet the Koran teaches that Iblis or Satan was cast out of heaven for his refusal to worship Adam (Sura 2:34; 7:11-13; 38:72-77). Wine is forbidden to Muslims here on earth (Sura 5:92, 2:219) but rivers of wine are promised them in Aljana, the Muslim heaven (Sura 47:15; 76:6; 83:25).

The true God is neither the author of confusion nor contradictions. These confusions and contradictions coupled with the historic blunders and errors may explain why Muslim scholars resist any serious analysis of the Koran.

In view of all the above, the question that comes to mind is this: "Who wrote the Koran?" Muslims believe that Allah sent the angel Gabriel at various times to dictate the Koran to Muhammad. Their reasoning is that Muhammad being an Ummie (i.e. illiterate), could not have written a book like the Koran by himself. At this juncture, it is wise to ask the following questions:

(1) Which university did our Lord Jesus attend?
(2) Prophet Noah (Nuhu), David (Dauda), Jonah (Yunus) etc. graduated from which academy?

---

[1] Editor's note: Suggesting that there are other gods besides Allah.

Illiteracy is neither synonymous with imbecility nor does it necessarily mean disability of the intellect nor lack of ingenuity. Educational qualifications are not the credentials for divine commission. But though Muhammad himself was illiterate, his advisers were not. Muhammad had some very able secretaries and religious advisers such as Zaid Ibn Thabit, a learned man who later headed the board of editors that edited the Uthmanic edition of the Koran (see page 20).

Before Jihad was declared against them, the people of Mecca were not taken in by Muhammad's "revelations." In many suras, the Koran itself records the Meccan allegation against Muhammad, that he forged the Koran with the help of other men:

> "But the misbelievers say: Naught is this but a lie which he has forged, and others have helped him in it . . ." (Sura 25:4; See also Sura 16:101, 103; 46:8).

The Meccans held on to that accusation until they were brutally overwhelmed by the bloody edge of the Islamic sword. Their accusations were not without merit. Muhammad did have a lot of editorial help.[1]

Unfortunately, men can condition themselves to believe in a fraud, if the fraud has existed long enough and is widely confessed, but there is no fraud in the Bible God. No matter how much a fraudulent religion is universally accepted, the verdict of Christ is:

> "Every plant [*religious system*] that my heavenly father has not planted will be pulled up by the roots:" (Matthew 15:13).

That is one of the reasons Jesus is coming again. He will descend like a furious eagle to tear to shreds all false religions and Satanic systems, for no foundation can stand apart from the one that is already laid, Christ Jesus, Himself:

> "For other foundation can no man lay than that is laid, which is Jesus Christ. Now if any man build upon this foundation [*of*

---

[1] Other advisers were: Waraqa ibn Naufal (Khadija's cousin). History has proved he was a Roman Catholic monk before pitching his tent with Muhammad as a religious adviser (cf. Yusuf Ali's Comm. No. 32). Abdullah ibn Salam, a learned Jewish rabbi before joining Muhammad. Others are Uthman Ibn Huwairith; Abu Faqaihah; a Greek renamed Abu Takbiha etc. (See Ibn Hisham, Siratu'r Rasul Vol. 1, p. 184; cf.. The Mizanul Haqq, Part 3, pp. 271, 272.).

Jesus with] gold, silver, precious stones, wood, hay, stubble; Every man's work shall be made manifest: for the [*last*] day shall declare it, because it shall be revealed by fire; and the fire shall try every man's work of what sort it is" (1 Corinthians 3:11-13)

Very soon you will be regretting in eternal fire unless you repent genuinely from your sins and accept Jesus with your whole heart and renounce the religion of the jinns.

Chapter 8

Satanic Verses in the Koran?

A time came in Islamic history when the Muslims faced severe persecution from the unyielding Meccans, so severe in fact, that eighty three of Muhammad's followers had to flee to Abyssinia (Ethiopia). When the persecution grew worse, Muhammad underwent a moment of despair and made compromising "revelations." He declared the possibility of Allah having a wife, Al-Lat and two daughters, Al-Uzza and Mannat, as recorded in Surat an-Najim:

> "For truly did he see, the signs of his Lord, the greatest! Have ye seen Lat, and Uzza, and another, the third [*goddess*] Manat? What! For you the male sex, and for him, the female? Behold, such would be indeed a division most unfair!" (Sura 53:18-22).

This indirect confession of polytheism made the Meccan pagans happy. Their bone of contention had been done away with (earlier, he had fearlessly lashed out against polytheism). The Meccans immediately lifted the boycott, stopped the persecution, and peace again reigned in Mecca. The Muslims who had migrated to Ethiopia heard the good news and returned home. But by then, Muhammad had withdrawn his confession. It appears that Muhammad realized the far reaching negative effect his compromise with the polytheists would have on his ministry. So on at least this one occasion, he admitted that he was actually inspired by Satan, as we read in Surat al-Hajj:

> "Never did we send an Apostle or a prophet before thee but when he frame a desire, Satan threw some [*vanity*] into his desire. But God will cancel anything [*vain*] that Satan throws in. And God will confirm [*and establish*] his signs. For God is full of knowledge and wisdom, that he may make the suggestions thrown in by Satan, but a trial. For those in whose hearts is a

disease and who are hardened of heart: Verily the wrong doers are in a schism far [*from truth*]" (Surat al-Hajj 22:52,53).

The Al-Jalalayn interpretation is that after Muhammad recited Surat an-Najim (Sura 53) before a Council, the angel Gabriel informed him that the verses *were put in his tongue by Satan*. Muhammad felt sorry and confessed his mistakes, supposing a similar fate befell preceding apostles.

Later on Allah annulled these Satanic verses with better "revelations." As the last part of verse 53 suggests, Allah supposedly permitted Satanic utterances to be in the Koran to test weak Muslims or to cut off those who had hardened hearts. Thus, Islam itself regards Sura 53:18-22 to be Satanic, and Muhammad did indeed reject them later. Remember Salman Rushdie? He didn't invent those Satanic verses. Those Satanic verses are really in the Koran.

Here is a serious point for Muslims to ponder:

So, provably, there was one occasion when Muhammad was unable to tell the difference between the voice of Satan and the voice of Allah. Is that the only time it happened? Could there be other revelations believed to be from Allah that were really from Satan? Is it possible that the whole Koran is little more than Satanic verses?

Muslims claim that the Koran contains the words of Allah, 100%, but the Koran not only has Satanic verses, but also a demonic sura. Unbelievably, a whole sura (chapter) in the Koran is named after the demons. Shocking but true. Sura 72 is entitled Jinn (demons), Here is a short quote:.

1. "Say: It has been revealed to me that a company of Jinns listened [*to the Koran*] They said, we have really heard a wonderful Recital!
2. It gives guidance to the right, and we have believed therein we shall not join [*in worship*] any [*gods*] with our Lord.
3. And exalted is the majesty of our Lord: He has taken neither a wife nor a son.
4. There are some foolish ones among us who used to utter extravagant lies against God.
5. But we do think that no man or spirit should say aught that is untrue against God.

6. True, there were persons among mankind who took shelter with persons among the jinns but they increased them in folly.

7. And they [came to] think as ye thought, that God would not raise up anyone [*to judgement*].

8. And we pried into the secret of heaven: but we found it filled with stern guards and flaming fires.

9. We used, indeed, to sit there in [*hidden*] stations, to [*steal*] a hearing: but any who listen now will find a flaming fire watching him in ambush.

10. And we understand not whether it is intended to those on earth or whether their Lord [*really*] intends to guide them to right conduct.

11. There are among us that are righteous and some the contrary: we follow divergent path.

12. But we think that we can by no means frustrate God, throughout the earth, nor can we frustrate Him by flight.

13. And as for us, since we have listened to the guidance, we have accepted it: and any who believes in his Lord has no fear, either of a short [*account*] or of any injustice.

14. Amongst us are some that submit their wills [*to God*] and some that swerve from justice. Now those who submit their wills–they sought out [*the path*] of right conduct.

15. But those who swerve, they are [*but*] fuel for hell fire."

It should disturb every Muslim that demonic conversations are considered to be part of the supposed word of Allah. But upon reflection you can see how and why they are.

First of all, let us define Jinns.

Advanced Learners Dictionary of Current English defined jinns to be genies or goblins – mischievous demons – ugly looking evil spirits. The Bible defines demons as angels who followed Satan in his rebellion against God:

"And there was war in heaven: Michael and his angels fought against the dragon; and the dragon fought and his angels, and prevailed not: neither was their place found anymore in heaven. And the great dragon was cast out, that old serpent, called the Devil, and Satan which deceiveth the whole world; he was cast out into the earth and his angels were cast out with him" (Rev. 12:7-9).

No one should take a jinn's claim seriously, that "some of them are righteous," Sura 72:11. Satan is the father of lies (John 19:44), so why should we believe what his Jinns said in the Koran? Jinns, like their Master (Satan), are liars. To deceive us, they gather half-baked truths into bundles of lies. That demons and Satan are barred from the true heaven forever is indicated from their own confession in verses 8-9. There they admit that they unsuccessfully tried to storm heaven but met opposition from stern-looking angelic guards. Even their attempt to spy at heaven was foiled as they admit in verse 9. The true nature and root of Islam is revealed in verse 14 when the jinns, (whom the Bible God cast out of heaven) became Muslims and found a refuge in Islam.

> "Among us [*jinns-demons*] are some that submit wills (to God) [*i.e. Muslims*] and some that swerve from justice. Now those who submit their wills [*demonic Muslims*] they sought out [*the path*] of right conduct." (Sura 72, Jinn, 14).

God forbid that I should belong to the same religion that the arch-enemies of God, the demons, also profess. Who could sponsor a religion that includes God's arch-enemies, i.e. the jinns (demons)? Only Satan posing as Allah would do so. Before their conversion, the evil spirits confessed what was later to be a central theme of Islam, that Allah has neither taken a wife nor had a son (72:3).

It is clear at this point that while posing as the angel Gabriel and claiming to be from Allah, one of these jinns (demons), gave Muhammad a denial of the sonship of Christ and the fatherhood of God. This blatant falsehood is repeated over twenty times in the Koran. Bearing in mind the Satanic verses incident, one must acknowledge that the devil can impersonate a holy angel. (2 Corinthians 11:13-15). As an interesting note, when Muhammad received his first "revelations," he was not sure of the source of them himself. His wife (Khadija) convinced him that they must have come by the angel Gabriel.[1]

Muhammad's encounter with the jinns (demons) is also recorded in another sura, Sura 46, Al-Ahqaf, 29-32:

> 29: "Behold, we turned towards the company of jinns [*quietly*] listening to the Koran; when they stood in thy presence thereof,

---

[1] See Yusuf Ali's Commentary No. 31-33.

they said 'Listen in silence!' when the (reading) was finished, they returned to their people, to warn [*them of their sins*].

30: They said, O our people! we have heard a Book revealed after Moses, confirming what came before it: It guides [*men*] to the truth and to straight path.

31: O our people hearken to the one who invite [*you*] to God, and believe in him: He will forgive you your faults, and deliver you from a penalty grievous.

32: If any does not hearken to the one who invites [*us*] to God, he cannot frustrate [*God's plan*] on earth, and no protectors can he have besides God; such men [*wonders*] in manifest errors.'"

These are admissions, within the Koran, that Muhammad had actual contacts with demons. This encounter is believed to have taken place at a time Muhammad lost his first wife, Khadija, and his uncle, Abu Talib, who had been protecting him all along. Muhammad tried to seek refuge in Taif, a village on the hilly side of Mecca, but the villagers rejected him, and he slipped out to the desert where the jinns (demons) met with him as he recited the Koran.

This second sura, dealing with the same event as in Sura Jinn, goes so far as to reveal that the jinns (demons), after listening to the Koran, began to proclaim it to others. In other words, demons became missionaries for Islam. Their support for the Koran shows that the jinns and Islam are inseparable. The conversion of seventy three Yatrib (Medina) pagans to Islam, before the Prophet Muhammad even set foot there, cannot be unconnected with the evangelistic activities of "faithful" jinns (demons). As expert whisperers, demons whispered to villagers, "Lo! we have heard a wonderful recitation, [*i.e. the Koran*], so believe it" (Sura 46:31). Obviously, demons played a crucial role in the formation of Islam, and today they are playing a significant role in its spread. The jinn's are true Muslims!

Chapter 9

Islam &
Christianity
on Idolatry

Most Muslims believe that Allah sent Muhammad to retrieve Christians from the error of Trinitarian polytheism. But before we respond to Allah's beckoning, don't we have the right to examine what we are being asked to believe? The Bible admonishes us to prove (examine) all things; and hold fast to that which is good (1 Thessalonians 5:21). Accepting a creed without examination and genuine conviction, is not just blind faith. It is like jumping from the frying pan to a roaring fire.

Unfortunately, our Muslim friends are in that exact position. Their ancestors were forced to embrace Islam at the point of the sword. Today, over 90% of the people in Islam were born into it and were then brainwashed through al-majirin (the local Islamic school indoctrination system). Through that system, they are given an anti-Gospel vaccination. They are nurtured from infancy with the idea that Christians worship three gods while they worship only one, Allah. Muslims accept this idea without further examination.

Any religion's claim about itself is not sufficient evidence of its validity. No religion (except Satanism) would admit outright that it is of Satanic origin, because no one would be lured into accepting it. Religion is like a letter written in the name of God. Examining the contents of the letter is necessary to determine whether it is of God or not. It is patently obvious that Christianity, Islam, Buddhism, Shintoism, Confucianism, Yogaism, Bahaism etc. – with their conflicting doctrines and confrontational postures – cannot all be from the same God. True God is not the author of confusion. A master stroke of Islam is its alleged teaching of one god – Allah – while declaring Christianity to be polytheistic. But do Muslims actually worship one god?

Muslims generally believe that the prophet Moses did speak directly with God, hence his Islamic title of Kalimullah. The first of the ten commandments God gave through Moses is:

> "Thou shalt not make unto thee any graven image, or any likeness of anything that is in heaven above or that is in the earth beneath, or that is in the water under the earth. Thou shalt not bow down thyself to them nor serve them". (Exodus 20:4-5).

The children of Israel often broke this commandment and most of their ordeals were a result of that sin. One of such instances is recorded in the book of Ezekiel:

> "He then brought me into the inner court of the house of the LORD, and there at the entrance to the temple, between the portico and the altar, were about twenty five men. With their backs towards the temple of the LORD and their faces towards the east, they were bowing down to the sun in the east" [*This Baal worship is similar to Islam*] (Ezekiel 8:15-16, NIV) .

The Children of Israel experienced the lovingkindness of Yahweh (God) in the wilderness; they witnessed His miracles. They knew it was not the sun in the sky that delivered them from Egypt, nor the sun that parted the Red Sea for them or provided them with manna during their wilderness wanderings. To the Israelites, the sun was but a symbol, and yet in the quote above they were bowing down to it. God who judges the intents of the heart, knew their hearts. He condemned their act and called it an abomination.

But what is the Islamic attitude towards a similar practice? Allah is alleged to have handed down the following command, as recorded in Surat al-Baqara:

> "From whencesoever thou startest forth, turn thy face in the direction of the sacred mosque, that is indeed the truth from thy Lord. And God is not unmindful of what ye do" (Sura 2:149).

And still in another verse, the same command is rendered thus:

> "We see the turning of thy face [*for guidance*] to the heavens: now shall we turn thee to a Qibla that shall please thee. Turn then thy face in the direction of the sacred mosque: whenever ye are, turn your faces in that direction" (Sura 2:144).

The reader should notice that Muslims were previously commanded to turn their faces towards Jerusalem when praying. What the speaker is saying in the above sura is that they should change to Mecca.

In the preface of the book entitled *Islam–The First and Final Religion*, page V, the author tries his best to defend the usual Islamic argument that Abraham and Ishmael built the Ka'aba for the worship of Allah.[1] Whether that claim is true or false is not the point. The Islamic Abraham is alleged to have been guilty of shirk (*idolatry*), so it is not surprising if it is also claimed that he built Ka'aba. That author went on to say that Muslims do not really worship or bow to Ka'aba, that the Ka'aba is only a symbol. That argument is not convincing at all. Why should anyone bow towards Ka'aba in the first place? If God detests bowing towards a sun that was made by Him, bowing towards a Ka'aba made by man would definitely be worse, even if it was built by Abraham. Is the command to face Ka'aba a test? (Sura 2:145). Does God test people with idolatry?

Why do Muslims run round the Ka'aba, and even go as far as kissing it during their "holy" pilgrimage?[2] History tells us that Arabian pagans performed this ritual before Islam. It is said that the first Khalifah of Islam, Abu Bakr, when kissing the black stone (of all the colors available under heaven, why they chose black is not without significance) said, "Of a truth, I know that you are nothing but a stone and can do nothing good or harm. Had I not seen the apostle of Allah kiss you, I would never kiss you" (Cf. Rafique, Kinsmen of Abraham, P. 19). Worthy of note is the fact that after the signing of the treaty of al-Hudybiyah (7 A.H.)[3] – while the Ka'aba was still housing those 360 idols – Muhammad performed the ritual pilgrimage to Mecca. The conquest of Mecca didn't take place for another year, (8 A.H.).

---

[1] Any Islamic claim of patriarchal accreditation for the Ka'aba would have been weak indeed, had it not been linked to Abraham, though there is no historic evidence at all that Abraham was ever in Mecca. The Ka'aba being linked to just Ishmael makes more sense, because Ishmael probably went into pagan idolatry after being driven from his father's house by God's command (Gen 21:10-14)

[2] The author is convinced that Ka'aba is the exact fulfilment of the image of the beast prophesied in Revelation chapter thirteen, verse fourteen.

[3] A.H. (After Hijra) is an Islamic way of reckoning time. A.H. time began in 622 AD, the year of Muhammad's flight (Hijra) from Mecca to Medina, a fulfillment of Daniel 7:25.

Muslims want the world to believe that the Ka'aba was sanctified (*purged*) because some of the physical idols were done away with. But religious matters go far beyond the physical world – powerful spiritual forces are involved. The Bible teaches that an idol is nothing in itself. What happens is that Satan stations demons (*jinns*) in venerated objects to influence people's minds. If you destroy the objects (*idols*), the demons (*jinns*), associated with those objects don't just vanish into thin air. Some demons are quite territorial, and will remain at the place where they were worshiped.[1] So what happened to the demons that stood behind idols that used to be at the Ka'aba? Who is in the Ka'aba now? Is it Allah, or some displaced jinns?[2]

Ask yourself, if Allah is omnipresent (i.e. present everywhere) why does one need to face in a particular direction to pray, and in the direction of a black stone for that matter?

"O ye who believe! intoxicants and gambling, [*dedication of*] stones and [*divination by*] arrows are an abomination, - of Satan's handiwork: eschew such [*abomination*], that ye may prosper" (Sura 5:93).

So the Koran teaches no dedication of stones, right? Well, what about the Ka'aba, which is also known as the black stone. If I were still a Muslim, I wouldn't know what to believe, because another "revelation" in the same Koran tells us that Ka'aba is not only to be venerated, but also the small hills of Safa and Marwa:

---

[1] Editor's Note: Though not generally understood in the United States, all false religions are demonically empowered. Demons (jinns) can even enable followers to perform supernatural phenomena: visions, different voices, unknown tongues, moving objects, levitation, calling up spirits, out-of-body experiences, death-curses, etc. The suicide bombers in Israel are demonically influenced to believe they are doing good, otherwise they would never perform such an unnatural act. Some pastors in the United States believe they see and speak to Jesus, but a biblical study of what their "angels" say to them shows their visions to be demonic. Scripture warns of this possibility, 2 Cor 11:14 "And no wonder, for even Satan disguises himself as an angel of light." Isn't seeing an "angel of light" what happened to Mohammed in that cave north of Mecca?

[2] Demons can be very territorial. Dr. Neil T. Anderson attests to this phenomenon in his book on freedom in Christ from demonic influence - Neil T. Anderson, *The Bondage Breaker* (Eugene, Oregon, USA, Harvest House Publishers, 1993) ISBN 0-89081-787-1.

"Behold! Safa and Marwa are among the symbols of God. So if those who visit the house [*Ka'aba*] in the season or at other times, should compass them round, it is no sin in them" (Sura 2:158).

Which symbol? Does Allah look like Ka'aba or Safa or Marwa? Historically, the idolatrous significance of these hills was so strong that early Muslims were reluctant to run round them at all. Hence the "revelation" sanctioning the practice. Since Allah also ordered the worship of a mere man, Adam (Sura 7:11-13; 38:72-77), his command for Muslims to venerate stones and hills should come as no surprise.[1]

What about the astrological symbol of crescent and star? How Islam came upon and accepted those occult symbols is best known only to Allah and his jinns. What about the string of beads that Muslims use in their prayers?

I used to be a Muslim, myself. My goal in this review of Islam is to point out the falsity of these abominations to unsuspecting worshipers. It is for the people who were made to memorize everything but have no way of knowing the truth or error of what they have learned. The aim of this book is achieved if, after reading it, you are (by God's grace), freed from this snare of the devil. Sacred hills, sacred stones and prayer beads are but institutionalized idolatry.

"Thou shalt not make unto thee any graven image . . . nor bow down to them." (Exodus 20:4).

---

[1] There is a reference in the Bible book of Zechariah that some believe to be about Islam and the Ka'aba. It is written in figurative language, but the intent of the passage is plain enough. Editor's notes within the Bible quote are in italics:

Zec 5:7-11 Again he said, "This is their appearance in all the land (and behold, a lead cover was lifted up); and this is a woman sitting inside the ephah *(Ephah was a son of Midian whose name meant "darkness." [See Holman's Bible Dictionary] An ephah may also be a small basket)*." Then he said, "This is Wickedness!" . . . And I said to the angel who was speaking with me, "Where are they taking the ephah *(the darkness or the basket of darkness?)*?" Then he said to me, "To build a temple for her in the land of Shinar *(in Zechariah's time, the Land of Shinar included Arabia)*; and when it is prepared, she will be set there on her own pedestal *(the Ka'aba?)*."

There is a now a pedestal in Mecca, dedicated to Allah, that all Muslims revere. And the people who worship Allah, are they not in great spiritual darkness?

"Thou" means everybody, including Abraham!

"And the rest of the men which were not killed by these plagues, yet repented not from the works of their hands that they should not worship devils, and idols of gold, and silver, and brass, and stones, and of wood; which neither can see, nor hear, nor walk; neither repented they of their murders, or of their sorceries, nor of their fornication nor of their theft" (Revelation 9:20-21).

Will ye not also repent? If you will not because you were born and bred in the religion, then hear the fate that awaits you:

"And the smoke of their torment ascended up for ever and they have no rest day nor night who worship the beast [*through false religions*] and his image . . ." (Revelation 14:11).

Some bow before the portrait of Jesus, Mary, a cross, or a crucifix. All such abominations carry severe punishments. Many so-called Christians also go on a pilgrimage to the Vatican to kiss the Pope's foot. This, too, is an abomination and without biblical support. Jesus repudiated the idea of pilgrimage. He stated that God, being a spirit, is everywhere. We may only worship Him in spirit and in truth.

"Jesus saith . . . believe me, the hour cometh, when ye shall neither in this mountain, nor yet at Jerusalem, worship the Father. Ye worship ye know not what: we know what we worship: for salvation is of the Jews. But the hour cometh, and now is, when the true worshiper shall worship the Father in spirit and in truth: for the Father seeketh such to worship him. God *is* a Spirit: and they that worship him must worship *him* in spirit and in truth" (John 4:21-24).

If we accept that kissing the foot of a man is abomination, then every right-thinking mind should admit that running round and kissing a lifeless structure as the Ka'aba is one of the worst abominations under the sun. Of a truth, religion outside Christ is religious paganism. False gods will always beget false prophets, and false prophets will in turn beget false religions.

Chapter 10

So who
is Allah?

Muslims use the remotest language possible to describe Allah. They try to make him as transcendent as possible in order to discourage people from conducting research on him. If you ask a Muslim to define Allah, he will just beat about the bush, ascribing attributes to him that neither belong to him nor befit him. But Allah is not as mysterious as Islam would like the world to believe. He has been at the Ka'aba stone all along. Certainly, Christians have not prayed enough to displace him and we may never do so until he meets his doom in the valley of Megiddo.

Some say that the word Allah was or is derived from the Syriac Alaha. But the name Allah was in existence long before Islam. That is evidenced from the name Abdullah (meaning servant of Allah) – the name of Muhammad's father. The question is this: To whom was this name originally revealed? Certainly none of the Biblical prophets ever referred to it. There is absolutely no trace of that name in the Bible. It is Arabic, not Israelite.

But in the mind of Islamic scholars, anything (negative or positive) done to further the cause of Islam is justifiable, so they can lie and claim that the name of Allah was revealed to Adam, Abraham or even Ishmael. Lies can be told about those patriarchs because they have been dead a long time and aren't around to refute any false claims. And they never leave Abraham alone.

In pre-Islamic Arabia, that Muslims now refer to as "Al-Jahiliya," meaning a period of ignorance, the Arabians were grossly paganistic. In and around Ka'aba, the Arabs worshiped 360 idols. Each clan had their own particular idols to worship. It is provable that Allah was one of the 360 idols that Muhammad's Hashimite clan worshiped.

Muhammad's grandfather, Abdul Muttalib, was the leader of Mecca and a custodian of Ka'aba's 360 idols. The Koran confirms that he was a pagan. The names that Muhammad's grandfather gave his children are further proof that Muhammad was from a family of idol devotees.

Muhammad's father was named Abdullah, meaning servant of Allah. The name of Muhammad's uncle was Abdul Manaf, meaning servant of Manaf. His other name was Abu Talib, meaning father of Talib. This is indisputable proof that Allah and Manaf were clannish idols worshiped by Muhammad and his people. Islamic scholars try to hide the historic fact that Muhammad worshiped idols before and after he claimed to be a prophet. But they can't do away with the record of the Koran itself.

That Muhammad was later fascinated by the monotheistic creed of Jews and Nestorian Christians is beyond question. He encountered many of them at Mecca and on his business trips to Syria. His wife, Khadija, was a Catholic, as was Waraqa ibn Naufal, his secret tutor.

Now, Muhammad wanted to unite the Arab race under a theocratic setting, but there was no way he could carry along all those 360 idols, so Muhammad decided to pick from among the idols of his clan. Naturally he picked Allah, the idol for which his father was named. Any of the idols would have served; an idol is an idol. It is the demon behind an idol that deceives the mind and heart.

Those who try to single out Allah and deify him above the other Meccan idols should remember that Muhammad could just as easily have picked Manaf, Al-Lat, Al-Uzza, or any of the others; and his choice didn't win the support of everyone, including his uncle, Abdul Manaf. That is clear from the fact that Abdul didn't submit to Allah and Islam until his death. He held on to Manaf.

This elevation of one idol over the other 359 angered the other Meccan clans. The purported persecution of Muhammad was nothing but an inter-tribal or inter-clannish quarrel over whose idol should be or whose should not be venerated. In the same vein, the Koran was written in Muhammad's dialect (Quraish). To pacify the other tribes, Muhammad told them (with concocted "revelations") that the preserved tablet in heaven was written in Quraish. The world was then asked to swallow the Islamic lie that all the Ka'aba idols were destroyed. It just isn't true. About four of those idols are said to remain. The custodians of Ka'aba should open the stone to independent inspectors should anyone dispute this.

Just as Islam led 1.2 billion Muslims and even some ignorant Christians to believe that Jesus is Isa or Esau, so it has tried to make the world believe that Allah is God. But there is no link between Allah and the Bible God, who revealed His name to be Yahweh, or the "I AM".[1]

Webster's New Collegiate Dictionary calls the name of the true God a "Tetragrammaton," which means that it is made up of four letters. Those Hebrew letters are transliterated YHWH or JHVH. They are usually pronounced Yahweh or Jehovah. Yahweh means the "I AM." That name defines God's eternal being and divine nature: The only true, almighty, personal, holy God, and "the Father of spirits" (Numbers 16:22, cf. John 4:24), The God who revealed Himself to His people, made a covenant with them, became their law giver, to Whom all honor and worship is due.

If God's name was really Allah, why didn't He give that name to the prophet Moses or to any of the other Old Testament prophets? Why didn't Jesus ever hint that God might have a name different than the one already revealed to the prophets? The Supreme Being is eternal isn't He? If God is without beginning or end, isn't His name also eternal and unchanging? Of course, but if the Koran is correct, then nobody knew God's name before Muhammad, and God didn't know what He was talking about when He told Moses that His name was "I AM that I AM."

It was at the burning bush that God revealed Himself to Moses as the "I AM" (Exodus 3:14). "I AM" portrays His eternal existence, with no beginning and no end. He is the only eternal God, there is no other. There is no room for any usurper idol, no matter what he calls himself. The name Allah does not belong to the true God, but to an Arabian idol.

But there is more. When Jesus called Himself "I AM" in John 8:58, He said in effect that He is the same "I AM" who spoke to Moses at the burning bush. The Jews understood exactly what Jesus meant, and tried to stone Him for it (John 8:59). They knew that Jesus was declaring Himself to be the final, perfect and practical revelation of true God. The prophet Isaiah knew it, too, when he called Jesus "Emanuel," meaning

---

[1] The etymological root of Yahweh is actually an unused Hebrew verb, *havah* (the verb to be). JHVH, the "I AM," appears in English Bibles as GOD or LORD, depending on the translation. The Jews today do not speak or write the word *havah,* say "I AM," or write the name of G-d in any form, because they consider the name of G-d too holy to utter or write. They leave out a letter in G-d, as you see here, or address Him as *Ha Shem,* which simply means "The Name."

"God with us." This is not polytheism, God the Father and Jesus His Son are one Being, one essence. Jesus said:

John 10:30 "I and My Father are One."

This is the only true and eternal God. All others are idols or imagined gods. [1]

I can hear some of you screaming, "Ha! That isn't so; Allah is just another name for God. Arabs worship the same God we do, under a different name."

That view is held by many misinformed people, but it is wrong. Granted, Allah is the Arabic term for their god, but is Allah the name of the sovereign and almighty God who created the universe? Aside from Muhammad (whose prophethood the Islamic scholars have yet to prove) there is no record anywhere on earth of God having spoken through Arabs. In fact, the Bible says just the opposite. The last book of the Bible was written at the end of the 1st century. One of its final statements is:

Rev 22:18 . . . If any man shall add unto these things, God shall add unto him the plagues that are written in this book.

Isn't that what Muhammad did? Didn't he claim to be a prophet long after God commanded that no one should add to His already revealed Word? So what does this prove, that an entire race can be wrong in their conception of deity? Well, the Bible says, "Let God be true, but every man a liar," (Romans 3:4). This means that anything written that is counter to God's Word is a lie. Since the supreme Being has told us that His name is Yahweh, the "I AM," whoever claims His name is something else has been influenced by the devil (John 8:44).

You would think Christians would distance themselves from anyone who believes that God didn't know His own name, but such is not the case. The Christians of Hausa stock worship and praise Allah. So long as Christians bow to Allah, victory over Islam will not happen. Little wonder that mission efforts among Muslims have had little effect. One who names

---

[1] Another verse in the Bible perfectly describes the oneness of Jesus the Son with God the Father, Isaiah 9:6 "For unto us a child is born, unto us a son is given: and the government shall be upon his shoulder: and his name shall be called Wonderful, Counsellor, The mighty God, The everlasting Father, The Prince of Peace."

the name of Christ and bows down to any false god, by whatever name, is just asking for the enemy to brand the number 666 on his forehead. Didn't Scripture forewarn us of this danger? Yes indeed:

"And he opened his mouth *(the dragon inspired beast)* in blasphemy against God, to blaspheme his name, and his tabernacle and them that dwell in heaven. And all that dwell upon the earth shall worship him, whose names are not written in the book of life of the Lamb slain from the foundation of the world." (Revelation 13:6, 8)

It is really blasphemy to slander the concept of the fatherhood of God and deity of Jesus Christ His Son. Those who do so, don't really know God. The above quote is very clear: everyone whose name is not written in Jesus' book of life is worshiping Satan (the dragon). The list of those in the dragon's clutches is endless. It includes Muslims, hypocritical Christians, Hindus, Buddhists, Hari Krishna, Rosicrucians, Satanists, drug addicts, homosexuals, rapists, pornographers, those who dabble into the occult and anyone else who turns away from Jesus, the Son of God.

Many Christians unwittingly worship the dragon in one way or the other. Some even sing choruses with Allah's name. If you call yourself a Christian and continue to revere Allah, then something is desperately wrong with your understanding of Christianity. The true God is a jealous God who will not tolerate the worship of any but Him. The Old Testament nation of Israel was destroyed because they worshiped other gods, and God has not changed. Maybe you are really sealed with Allah's seal – with a "666" on your forehead, or maybe your name is not in the Lamb's book of life – a Christless Christian – worshiping the dragon. (Rev. 13:8).

Some yet argue that the Allah the Christians worship is different from the Allah of the Muslims. They say that Christians and Muslims differ in their understanding of the character of Allah. But who has a greater claim to Allah than the Muslims, and how many Allah's are there? Many who call themselves Christians are a kind of Rachel in Christian disguise.[1] In the same way, many so-called Christians who don't have a correct understanding of the God of the Bible go a-whoring after the Islamic god of Allah. They use every argument under heaven to justify their spiritual

---

[1] Rachel, due to her lack of a personal knowledge of the "I AM," stole her father's idol, Gen. 31:19.

bankruptcy, but to no avail. Arguments that do not agree with God's Word, no matter how logical they may seem, will only lead to strong delusion.

> "And with all deceivableness of unrighteousness in them that perish; because they received not the love of the truth, that they might be saved. And for this cause God shall send them strong delusion, that they should believe a lie." (2Thess. 2:10-11)

The translators of the Hausa Bible have aggravated the problem. They substituted the name Allah for Yahweh, thereby bringing many Christians under the influence of the dragon. Some are of the opinion that before the name "Allah" was used in the Hausa Bible, scholars must have done extensive research to support their position. But no kind of research excuses an inaccurate Bible translation. God knew what His name was when He inspired the Bible, and He gave nobody the authority to change it. Truth is not discovered through human research, no matter how scholarly, but by divine enlightenment through the exact Word of God. Rest assured that any Bible translator who confused Allah with Yahweh was not inspired by God to do so.

The Origin of Islam among the Hausas

How did the Hausa come about the name "Allah" in the first place? Well, Sunni Islam came to the Hausa people in the fourteenth century through the influence of Sudanic and Arab merchants. However, the purity of that Islam was questioned by a Fulani speaking scholar and religious leader, Uthman Dan Fodio, who in 1802 declared Jihad against the traditional Hausa rulers, replacing the indigenous Hausa aristocracy with a Fulani feudalism. [1]

---

[1] Islamic purity was merely a pretext. The underlying aim of the Jihadists was to foist Fulani imperial hegemony on the people of Africa south of the Sahara. The usual tactic of Islam is to use their religion for political gain. That is clearly seen in the overthrow of the Hausa kingship. The Sokoto caliphate, with its emirate system entrenched in almost all parts of Northern Nigeria was able to enslave a whole race. The Islam entrenched at the end of Uthman Dan Fodio's revolution was no different from the Islam it supposedly purged. Neither is the present Islam as practiced by the descendants of Uthman Dan Fodio different from the Islam of the time of the Hausa kings. Islam is the only system where the enslaved do not aspire for freedom because the masters tell their victims that it is the will of Allah. This is why there will never be democracy in the Arab world. And the West will

Hausa men of today not only worship Allah but think, eat, drink and talk Allah so much so that the pre-Islamic name for the supreme being has been all but lost. Many people including some Christians are ready to argue at length that Hausas have had no other name for God but Allah. Some even argue that Allah is an Hausa word. They are pitifully wrong. Before Islam was introduced to the Hausas in the 14th century, the Hausa name for the supreme being was "Ubangiji." That is a truth that many Hausa men can still confirm.

So why was Allah substituted for Ubangiji? No one really knows. But it is Arabic, and Arabic is the language of Islam.[1] All Muslims are taught to revere Arabic above their native tongues and Arabic is learned and memorized by all. Arabic is so revered by some Muslims that they even drink a concoction called "Ruwa Alo" (made by washing verses of the Koran written on a slate – a superstition that is believed to be medicinal). The simple confession of Islamic faith, "Lahi la illa llah Muhammadu rasul la llah"[2] may have knocked the Hausas' pre-Islamic name for God out of

---

always look the other way. That Uthman Dan Fodio's hidden agenda was colonialism is unquestionable – he gave out flags to lieutenants who moved into various parts of Nigeria for settlement. They then fueled inter-tribal feuds in those areas. The Fulanis pretended to play the role of peace makers, or like the case of Ilorin, they waged war with the natives to break off from the yoke of the Alafin in Oyo empire. Subsequently, they killed off these tribal heads and seized power in the confusion. They even attacked the Borno empire, which was not only an Islamic state but had refined scholars like El-Kanemi as their leaders.

[1] It should be rightly termed racism. Aside from Arabic, other languages considered holy in Nigeria are those of the early Jihadists, their collaborators or victims; Fulfulde, Hausa, Kanuri. Anyone who wants to fit into the system must speak these languages. Through this radical Islamic racism many tribal languages have been obliterated, such as Holma and Zunu. These were prominent languages in Adamawa region, but they are no longer spoken. The Fulanis who brought Islam to them told them their languages were an abomination and paganistic, but that the Fulfulde and Hausa languages were holy.

To join the Kanuri/Borno political system and enjoy the privileges of the state, quite a number of tribes are disowning their languages. By the time they identify with Fulani, Kanuri or Hausa, they are enmeshed in Islam. People groups like the Galgamas, Kotokos, and others prefer to be known as Kanuris, not because they want to be, but because they feel insecure, and unaccepted as themselves.

[2] "Lahi la illa llah Muhammadu rasul la llah" literally means: No god but the god and Muhammad is messenger of the god.

their language. That confession has no room for Ubangiji. Perhaps the name "Ubangiji" was dropped to avoid any appearance of "polytheism."

The Koran has always been used as a vehicle for exporting Arab imperialism; conquered countries becoming vassal states of the caliphate. Arab methods may have softened some over time, but their goals remain the same: world conquest for Islam with an Arabian flavor. Egypt is a case in point. Egypt today is more Arabian than Egyptian. In His book, *Black Gold and Holy War*, PP. 8-9, Ishak Ibrahim, an Egyptian national, paints a rather bleak picture of how the Arabs invaded his country and then permeated Egypt with their culture:

> "These latter invaders *(the Arabs)* not only occupied Egypt like the previous powers but through their cultural imperialism permeated every area of Egyptian life, becoming within a few years an integral part of it. The change they wrought was permanent. Egypt's original heritage was never to be seen again except dimly in the lives of a small minority of Coptic Christians who refused total submission to the Arab enslavers. The high cost of refusal often meant their own death. Through manipulation, blackmail and outright obliteration of resistance, Islam became the religion of the majority in Egypt. Few people were asked to pay the high taxes (Jizya) the Arabs imposed, so their only alternative (if they wanted to live) was to accept Islam, to become 'part of the faithful'. Those too poor to pay taxes, yet unwilling to convert to Islam, were martyred."

That is the Islamic method, with the ordinary man-on-the-street forced into a satanic – convert or die – religious web. The ordinary Muslim desperately needs our love and prayers. He needs to be freed from the satanic bondage to which he was unwillingly enslaved. We must repent of wishing him ill. I know what I am talking about, because I've been there. I used to be a Muslim.

Many Christians in Nigeria, especially those in the north, are not interested in reaching Muslims. Clergy and laity alike are of the opinion that Muslims should die and go to Hell for killing Christians and burning their churches. I believe such Christians are more wicked than the Muslims they condemn.

Truly speaking, Muslims are not wicked. What people see as wickedness is religious fervor. They try as hard as they can to live by what they believe. Muslims are not only ready to kill for Islam but to die for it – a lesson, indeed, to those who say they believe in Jesus but are not ready to make any sacrifice for Him.

The aversion towards Muslim people is everywhere. An American missionologist, conducting a survey in Egypt, found that Coptic Christians (after 1,300 years of severe persecution from Islam) were against the salvation of Muslims. The Coptics believe it would be grossly unfair for Muslims to be saved and make it to heaven after enjoying everything they have on earth at the expense of others.

We need to take to heart the example of Nelson Mandela of South Africa. After being incarcerated for almost three decades by the supporters of Apartheid, he pardoned all those who jailed him, blaming nobody but the system. Likewise we need to love Muslims but hate the demonic Islamic system by which they are bound. We are not instructed to fight human beings but the devil, not with physical weapons, but with the weapons of God's Word and prayer (Ephesians 6:12). Love that does not reach out to help those that are hurting is not God's kind of love. (See Matthew 5:44).

I am convinced that if Jesus was physically present now, He would not be going to the churches, but to mosques, to bring Muslims into the kingdom. His parable in Luke 15:3-7 sets the example. Jesus didn't come to save the righteous, but to bring sinners to repentance. Open the Bible, read it, and fall upon your knees. We need to ask God to forgive us for our hardened hearts and our negligence.

Chapter 11

Islam & the Status of Women

Islam has much to say about the status of women. The Koran is said to have so exalted women that a whole sura, Sura an-Nisa, is named after them. But the real question is this: what exactly does that sura teach? The sura in Ayat 3 i.e. Sura 4:3, permits Muslims to marry as many as four wives at one time and a man may divorce them ("if need be") and marry a whole new set of wives at random. Christians believe that God could have created a host of wives for Adam if polygamy had been in God's original plan. But He only gave Adam one wife, and Eve became "the mother of all living" (Genesis 2:22; Matthew 19:4-6; 1 Corinthians 7:2).[1]

While there is a ceiling on the number of wives a Muslim can have at one time, there is no limit on the number of concubines he may accumulate (Sura 4:24 cf. Sura 33:50). It seems that the economic position of a man determines the number of concubines he may have. The appropriate definition of concubinism is legalized adultery and prostitution. Adultery is defined as a married person having sexual intercourse with someone other than his wife, while a concubine is a woman not married to a man but living with him as if she were his wife. In the light of the Bible, a man that keeps concubines is an

---

[1] The Bible goes on to say: Gen 2:24 "Therefore shall a man leave his father and his mother, and shall cleave unto his wife: and they shall be one flesh." Note that wife is stated in the singular, it is not wives. A man becomes one flesh with one wife. God hates divorce for any reason: Mal 2:14-16 "Because the LORD hath been witness between thee and the wife of thy youth, against whom thou hast dealt treacherously: yet is she thy companion, and the wife of thy covenant . . . Therefore take heed to your spirit, and let none deal treacherously against the wife of his youth. For the LORD, the God of Israel, saith that he hateth divorce: for one covereth violence with his garment, saith the LORD of hosts: therefore take heed to your spirit, that ye deal not treacherously."

adulterer while women in that position are but whores and prostitutes. Yet Islam and Allah condone these gross immoralities.[1]

Are you still wondering why Islam is opposing the Bible? If Islam is not a system of inequality and partiality, why does it not permit women to be married to four men at a time and allow them to have as many male concubines as they wish? If adultery can be legalized for men, why isn't it legalized for women as well? After all, what is good for the gander should also be good for the goose. I know however, that men, being what they are, would never accept such an arrangement. I would be filled with indignation if another man used my wife. Women feel the same way, even if they do not express it.

A Muslim can refuse to have relations with his wives if they misbehave (no thanks to the chain of concubines he is entitled to keep). A man can physically beat his wives if rebellion persists (Sura 4:34). A women guilty of lewdness (adultery) is to be locked up in prison until she dies (Sura 4:15), while a man, guilty of the same offence, just has to repent to regain his freedom. (Sura 4:16).

Legal Status of Women

A husband and wife together give direction and purpose to their family. However, in Islam, the wife is not even close to being an equal partner with her husband. He is a demigod in the house, who holds all rights and authority in his hands. The children are legally his.

He does meet the needs of his family , but is required to tell them nothing about his financial condition. The wife is not necessarily a lifetime companion with equal rights, but is looked upon as a "guinea pig" for sexual experimentation or as a baby mill.

There are exceptions of course, where noble and sensitive Muslims open up to the influence of worldwide human rights campaigners or where some astute wives exert control over their husbands. Christendom

---

[1] Prophet Moses recorded in the Ten Commandments: Exo 20:14 "Thou shalt not commit adultery." Commandments against fornication and adultery are repeated again and again throughout the Bible, for instance: 1 Cor 6:18 "Flee fornication. Every sin that a man doeth is without the body; but he that committeth fornication sinneth against his own body." Fornication is defined as having sexual intercourse with anyone other than your own wife.

has also influenced Arab customs to some degree. But in general, it is clear that Islam is a man's world. Women must stay in the background.

In a law court, the testimony of a man is equal to that of two women. If a family inheritance is involved, a female beneficiary always receives less than a male. In fact, the Koran directs: "To the male a portion equal to that of two females" (Sura 4:11; 4:176).

The Koran beautifully sums up women's status in Surat al-Baqara: "your wives are as tilth (farmland) unto you; so approach your tilth when or how ye will" (Sura 2:223). To say that wives must be passive partners is an understatement. According to the Koran they are like farmlands or landed properties while the husbands are husbandmen. As farmlands have no will of their own, in Islam, neither do wives.

American or Western ladies who are driven by hormones to marry Muslim immigrants should count the cost before jumping into such an arrangement. So-called "infidel" women who, in the heat of the moment, have married Muslim men, now regret that decision at leisure.

Does Koran recognize the prophethood of women?

The Bible recognizes the fact that it is the spirit and not the sex that counts in the service of God hence the Bible gives room for women prophets (*prophetesses*), women teachers and evangelists, just as men. We learned from Exodus 15:20, that Miriam, the sister of Moses and Aaron, was a prophetess. The Koran, while teaching that Moses and Aaron were prophets, refuses to recognize Miriam as a prophetess because Islam cannot imagine a woman occupying the office of a prophet. The Bible again recognized Anna, daughter of Phanuel as a prophetess (Luke 1:36).[1]

Just as Abraham was singled out for his faith (Genesis 15:6 cf. Rom. 4:3), so his wife (Sarah) was commended among women for her obedience (1 Peter 3:6). The Bible is full of women activists, Queen Esther

---

[1] Editor's Note: In the New Testament era, there are scriptural limits on when a woman may minister. If Christian brethren are present she is to remain quiet and be in submission. "But I suffer not a woman to teach, nor to usurp authority over the man, but to be in silence" (Ti 2:11-12). That command is reinforced by "Let your women keep silent in the churches" (i.e., when the church meets as a mixed gender body of believers, 1Co 14:34). This injunction is not placed on women because of inequality before the throne of grace, but that the type of Christ and the Church may not be broken (Eph 5:21-32 cf. 1Co 11:2-6). See E. Skolfield, *Demons in the Church* (Fort Myers, FL, Fish House, 1993)

being an example (read the Bible book of Esther). There were many others: Tabitha or Dorcas (Acts 9:36); Lydia (Acts 16:14-15); Phoebe, the deaconess (Roman 16:1). The list is endless, in short the Bible goes to a great length to make no spiritual distinction between man and woman. We are all one in Christ Jesus (Galatians 3:28). It is this spirit of equality that allows women to worship in the same church alongside their male counterparts.

In this part of the world, Muslim women are not permitted to pray in the same mosque along side men. When a renowned Islamic scholar vowed some time ago that he would not live to see a women president of this nation, he was merely displaying the Islamic spirit. In Pakistan, a general outcry greeted the election of Mrs. Benazir Bhutto (later ousted by referendum), but she was only being treated in accordance with the Islamic view of a woman's status. Maybe Allah will create a separate Aljana for women.

I truly sympathize with Muslim women. There is no way for them to get free of their servitude as long as they remain in Islam. Of a fact, Islamic law and family ties make it more difficult for Muslim women to shake off their shackles than in any other society on earth. However, there is hope for you when you turn to Christ. His blood can melt away all the chains of oppression and bondage.

Chapter 12

Moral Life of Prophet Muhammad

The Christian refusal to recognize the prophethood of Muhammad is annoying to most Muslims. They wonder why we fail to reciprocate their recognition of the prophethood of Jesus. Our Muslim friends should be aware of the fact that the recognition of a true prophet is not based on mutual approval. If Muhammad was the "greatest" and the "seal" of the prophets – if he provides a more sure and certain way of getting to heaven than Jesus does – then Christians should not hesitate to accept him. But a thorough investigation of a prophet must take place before he is received, because believing a prophet's message can have eternal consequences for our souls.

During the course of our investigation, we should also be permitted to question a prophet's morality, and this includes Muhammad's. As the "Seal" of the prophets (an Islamic claim), and according to the Koran, Muhammad was granted a special marital status by Allah. Many Islamic historians admit that Muhammad married eleven wives. Those who think his escapades with women a measure of his greatness, admit that he had as many as twenty seven. In addition to these wives, Muhammad was also commanded by Allah to keep as many concubines (female captives in Jihad) as his right hand possessed. Pondering the Koranic text that granted these special privileges to Muhammad, one cannot resist the temptation to believe that Muhammad wanted the unrestricted freedom to have as many women as he wished, and used his "revelations" to prevent his wives and followers from placing any limitations on his carnal cravings. That is not just an idle speculation:

The following "revelations" speak for themselves:

"O prophet! We have made lawful to thee thy wives to whom thou hast paid their dowers; and those whom thy right hand possesses out of the prisoners of war whom God, has assigned to thee; and daughters of thy paternal uncles and aunts, and daughters of thy maternal uncles and aunts who migrated [*from Mecca*] with thee; and any believing woman who dedicates her soul to the prophet if the prophet wishes to wed her; – this only for thee, and not for believers [*at large*]; we know what we have appointed for them as to their wives and the captives whom their right hand possess; – in order that there should be no difficulty for thee. And God is oft-forgiving, most merciful" (Sura 33:50).

With fleets of wives at Muhammad's disposal, coupled with his special privilege to have as many concubines as he desired, Muhammad's passion for women seemed to know no bounds. He even took the only wife of his adopted son, Zaid. Zaid Ibn Haritha was Muhammad's freed man and adopted son. Muhammad wedded Zaid to a beautiful lady named Zainab, but with the passage of time, Muhammad's heart began to long for her. So on his visit to Zaid's abode, the prophet of Islam said: "Praise belongeth unto Allah who turneth the hearts of men as he willeth." Zaid got the message and arranged to divorce his wife.

Muhammad knew quite well that nothing short of a new "revelation" could save his face from this detestable act, so he dissuaded Zaid from putting his wife away until the transaction could be sanctioned by a "revelation" from Allah. Read the words of the following sura:

"Behold! thou didst say to one who had received the grace of God and thy Favor: 'retain thou [*in wedlock*] thy wife, and fear God.' But thou didst fear in thy heart that which God was about to make manifest: thou didst fear the people, but it is more fitting that thou shouldest fear God. Then when Zaid had dissolved [*his marriage*] with her, with the necessary [*formality*], we joined her in marriage to thee: in order that in [*the future*] there may be no difficulty to the believers in [*the matter of*] marriage with the wives of their adopted sons, when the later have dissolved with the necessary [*formality*] [*their marriage*] with them. And God's command must be fulfilled." (Sura 33:37)

The reason for these self-serving "revelations" is obvious: Zainab, daughter of Jahsh, was Muhammad's cousin, and the Arabian custom (before

Islam) forbade marriage with the wives of their adopted sons even after divorce.[1] Can you imagine a religion that claims to promote purity of heart and good moral conduct, permitting its prophet – who already had eleven wives plus numerous concubines – to take the only wife of his own adopted son? The pathetic side of this recorded historic incident is that Allah, supposedly the architect of justice and morality, actually approved of this despicable act. The doom of all who love justice, holiness and righteousness is sealed if Allah, who condones this kind of wickedness, is allowed to prevail.

On the other hand, the God of the holy Bible is against sin of any kind, and will punish whoever commits it. There is no respect of persons with the God of the Bible (Romans 2:11). If the Bible God were to be the same as the Koranic Allah, then He would have to apologize for punishing the prophet David, who fell into a similar sin (2 Samuel 12:1-12). Letters of apology would also need to be dispatched to the people of Sodom and Gomorrah, whom God destroyed for immorality (Genesis 19:24-28).

While the Bible teaches that God is all powerful, it also teaches that He is absolutely holy. The Bible God cannot exercise His power in a way that contradicts His holy nature. The Christian God always acts in accord with His holiness. The Bible God has never tolerated sin. If He did, He would cease to be a holy God. That was why He cast Satan and his fallen angels out of heaven. That is why He punished Noah's generation, Sodom and Gomorrah and the rest.

One of Islam's major ills is a faulty concept of God. Islam sees God as a very powerful being who exercises his power capriciously. Who can question him, they reason. Whereas the Bible God changes not. He is the same, yesterday, today and forever.

Another example of prophet Muhammad's moral life is his affair with Maryam – a Coptic girl presented to him by the governor of Egypt. He slept with her on the day it was Hafsah's turn. In an attempt to defuse Hafsah's anger, Muhammad swore never to touch the girl again. He then commanded Hafsah to keep the matter secret from his other wives. However, she disclosed the matter to them. Displeased at finding his confidence betrayed, Muhammad disciplined the rest of his wives by

---

[1] Comp. Yusuf Ali's Comm. No. 3726

separating from them for one month, a time incidentally, which he spent in Maryam's apartment. Call it a temporary divorce!

As expected, "revelations" poured down from Aljana. The revelations not only favored Muhammad but also contained assurances of backing from Allah, Gabriel, righteous believers and the angels:

> "O Prophet! why holdest thou to be forbidden that which God has made lawful to thee? Thou seekest to please thy consorts [*wives*] but God is oft-forgiving, most merciful. When the Prophet disclosed a matter in confidence to one of his consorts [*wives*], and she then divulged [*to another*], and God made it known to him, he confirmed part thereof and repudiated a part. Then when he told her thereof, she said 'who told thee these?' He said 'He told me who knows and is well acquainted [*with all things*]? If ye two turn in repentance, to Him, your hearts are indeed so inclined; but if ye back up each other against him, truly God is his protector, and Gabriel, and [*every*] righteous one among those who believe, – and furthermore the angels will back [*him*] up'" (Sura 66:1,3,4).

As can be seen from the following Ayat, the Koran went on to absolve Muhammad of any guilt in the incident, and to free him from censure if similar cases were to arise in the future:

> "It may be, if he divorced you [*all*], that God will give him in exchange consorts [*wives*] better than you, – who submit [*their wills*], who believe, who are devout, who turn to God in repentance, who worship [*in humility*], who travel [*for faith*] and fast, – previously married or virgins" (Sura 66:5).

Let's look at the incident honestly. Maryam who was at the center of this episode was not legally married to Muhammad. Her position was that of a concubine. Muhammad lay with her on the day due Hafsah, and Allah, who is supposedly just in his judgement, or at least considerate, is portrayed as sending down verdicts against Muhammad's wives for daring to raise their eyebrows at his actions. However, another contradiction arises here. Other "revelations" represent Allah as telling Muhammad to pray for the forgiveness of his sins:

"Verily, we have granted thee a manifest victory: that God may forgive thee thy faults of the past and those to follow; and guide thee on the straight path" (Sura 48:1-2).

Commentator Abbasi explains this to mean the offences which Muhammad committed before he claimed to be a prophet, and those that he was going to commit even until his death. Imam Al-Zamakhshari, in his commentary says: "What went before of thy fault; i.e. the matter of Zainab, and what followed after; i.e. the matter of Maryam (Mary the Copt)." The meaning of the Glorious Koran (Pickthall translation) rendered Sura Muhammad, 19 thus:

"So know (O Muhammad) that there is no God save Allah, and ask forgiveness for thy sin and for believing men and women, Allah knoweth [*both*] your places of turmoil and your place of rest" (Sura 47:19).

The Hadiths also pictured Muhammad as conscious of his sins, thereby pleading for pardon.[1]

In the Koran, in every case where Muhammad's actions are questionable, Allah justifies his actions with "revelations." Muhammad's affair with Zainab (his son's wife) is an example. Even Arabian pagans regarded that behavior as an abomination. But, surprisingly enough, it got the blessing of Allah whose standards of morality were supposedly higher than those of Arabian pagans. Allah also supported Muhammad in his liaison with Maryam, the Copt. Justifying Muhammad's behavior while commanding him to ask forgiveness for his sins leaves room for another possibility: that Muhammad had committed graver sins (not recorded in the Koran) for which Allah is telling him to ask pardon.

How Muhammad Treated His Opponents

A general misunderstanding of the Islamic world by western nations is causing serious international tensions. Whenever the Islamic faithful carry out their religious duties, they are tagged as terrorists. Americans are so obsessed with the term "terrorist" that their government has blacklisted a number of Islamic countries: Libya, Iran and Syria.

---

[1] See Mishkatul Masabih, p. 62

When Islamic suicide bombers, May 15 group, Abu Nidal, Hamas, Islamic brotherhood, Mujahadin, Hisbollah, etc. carry out their religious obligation against Israeli civilians, those who are ignorant of the elementary principles of Islam call them all sorts of names. Those who know nothing about Muhammad's writings are baffled when they hear that the above mentioned groups have guerillas, assassins, kidnappers and weapon experts all over the world, including within the United States itself. It is beyond Western understanding that a seemingly logical people proudly take credit for blowing up airborne planes (with hundreds of innocent souls aboard), and other wanton murders, plus the destruction of their property.

Why should a seemingly sane people choose violence, anarchy, war and murder as a way of life, and even anticipate more of the same in Aljana? Part of the answer lies in the way and manner that Muhammad, the prophet of Islam, treated his opponents. During his lifetime, Muhammad sent assassin after assassin (today we call them "death squads") to eliminate his opponents. He rained curses upon the ones his assassins couldn't track down. Here are a few examples:

Muhammad sent Umayr b. Adi (Allah's helper) to kill Asthma bint Marwan, a poetess who wrote against him. The assassin entered the woman's abode at night and found her surrounded by her sleeping children, including a suckling child whom he pushed away from her breast. He then drove his sword through her body, murdering her.

In another dreadful incident, Muhammad sent Salim b. Amir to assassinate a 120 year old Jew whose poetry attacked Muhammad. On hot summer nights, the Jew would sleep in the courtyard of his home. Salim knew that, so he sneaked in and plunged his sword into the old man's liver, killing him.

It is related by Ibn Hisham (quoting Ibn Ishaq) that Muhammad said, "Whomsoever among the men of the Jews you overcome, kill him." That was enough incitement for Muhaisah ibn Mas'ud, who subsequently attacked and killed ibn Shunaimah, a Jewish merchant.

The story of the murder of Ka'b ibnu'l Ashraf is told in Ibn Hisham's Siratur Rasul vol. 2, p. 25. Ka'b ibnu'l Ashraf returned to Medina and praised the beauty of Muslim wives until the Muslims were annoyed. The Apostle of Allah said, "Who is with me in the matter of Ibnu'l Ashraf?"

Muhammad ibn Malamah replied, "I am for thee in this affair, O Apostle of Allah: I will kill him". He laid in ambush for three days, neither eating nor drinking until, with the assistance of five assassins, he killed Ka'b ibnu'l Ashraf.

Muhammad appointed five other assassins, Abdullah ibn utaik, Masud ibn Sanan, Abdullah ibn Unais, Abu Quadatu'l Harith ibn Rab'i and Khaza'i ibn Utaik, to go to Khaiba to murder Abi'l Huqaiq. The deed was carried out successfully, to the supposed glory of Allah.

On another occasion, Muhammad praised Zaid for commanding the brutal murder of an aged woman named Umm Kirfa. Her legs were tied to camels. These were driven in different directions until the unfortunate woman was torn asunder.

Muhammad also sent 'Amr ibn Umayyah and jabbar ibn Sakhar from Medina to Mecca to assassinate Abu Sufan ibn Harb. However, those hired killers failed in their mission because the plot was uncovered before they were able to strike. (Ibn Hishan Siratur Rasul vol. 3, pp.89,90).

Some escaped Muhammad's hit squads, but they could not escape his venomous outbursts. Since in Islam, love and mercy are regarded as weaknesses, Muhammad was not expected to pardon those who offended him. Vendetta is an extolled virtue in Islam. Listen to this one of the suras of Koran that many Muslims believe supersedes the Holy Bible:

> Perish the hands of the Father of Flame! Perish he! No profit to him from all his wealth, and all his gains! Burnt soon will he be in a fire of blazing flame! " His wife shall carry the (crackling) wood – as fuel! – A twisted rope of Palm - leaf fibre around her (own) neck!" (Sura 111:1-5).

This sura is dedicated solely to the cursing of one of Muhammad's uncles, Abu Lahab, meaning father of Lahab, but nicknamed father of flame because he rejected Muhammad's prophetic claims.

Since Muslims believe that every word, comma, semi-colon, full stop, in the Koran is the word of Allah, we should take the above sura as a "revelation" from him. It proves further that Allah has no love, no mercy and no forgiveness, only cursing, killing, wars and judgment.

The indiscriminate assassination of people throughout the world by Islamic faithfuls is nothing new. They are merely imitating the prophet Muhammad who, after all, is the "perfect" model of correct Islamic behavior. Ignorance of Islam is what makes western journalist call Islamic faithfuls "terrorists".

However, so-called terrorism is just what we see in the physical world. It is not the real problem. What we really have between Islam and the West is a titanic but unseen spiritual battle that began in the garden of Eden. It is a conflict between God and Satan, love and hatred, good and evil, peace and war. Those battle-lines are clearly visible now. The peace of Khalifah Haroun al-Rashid is over, and a militant Islam again calls for a worldwide Jihad. [1]

---

[1] Editor's Note: The first Islamic Jihad ended in 786AD, when Khalifah Haroun al-Rashid made peace with the Western nations. From then until this very century, Islam remained primarily in the Middle East, and as a minority religion in Africa and the Far East. Islam did not again pose a threat to world peace until after WW2, when the West started sending vast sums of money to the Arab nations in exchange for oil. That oil money has enabled the Middle East (the Leopard-Bear-Lion beast of Revelation 13:1-9) to arm itself with modern weaponry. In those figurative verses, the Bible clearly predicts there would be a 2nd Islamic Jihad just prior to Jesus' return. That 2nd Jihad is visible today in the military and economic pressure with which the Islamic states and the Palestinians are threatening Israel and the West.

Revelation further shows that this Jihad would lead to Earth's final war, the battle of Armageddon (Rev 16:12-16). Though Armageddon may spread over the whole world, with up to 2,500,000,000 people killed, it will begin in the Middle East and be of short duration. It will end with the return of the Lord Jesus. For further details, see Ellis H. Skolfield, *SOZO, Survival Guide for a Remnant Church*, (Fish House Publishing, Ft. Myers, FL, 1995)

Chapter 13

Jihad

JIHAD literally means "a great striving," and that striving includes a relentless and remorseless worldwide aggression. Jihad is a multi-action form of warfare, a more "total" war than that practiced by the fascist and Communist leaders of this century. Jihad does call for armed struggle and battle, but it also means a war through subversion and propaganda, through conversion of non-Muslims to Islam, and penetration of non-Muslim societies. Political and economic pressure is involved, such as the cutting off of oil supplies or the buying of property in "target" countries.[1] Western lands beware! For instance, Arab nations, particularly Saudi Arabia, now have significant holdings in the United States and other western countries, all bought with western oil money.

How did it all begin? Well, Muhammad's attempt to persuade his tribesmen to embrace his teachings by peaceful means only brought him threats, mocking and severe persecution. But Muhammad's persecution did not arise from his advocating the worship of Allah. Allah had been worshiped by his people for centuries. Historically, Allah was one of the 360 gods on display in Ka'aba. Going by his name, which means "servant of Allah," Muhammad's father, Abdullah, was probably a priest of Allah. The Meccans were provoked because Muhammad appeared to be staging a religious coup d'etat in favor of only one of their 360 idols at the Ka'aba, namely Allah. They couldn't understand why Muhammad should elevate that one idol above the other 359.

That was the primary cause of Muhammad's flight (Hijra) from Mecca to Medina (then Yatrib) in 622 AD. From the passages of the Koran

---

[1] This was put into practice during the Yom-Kippur-Jihad against Israel on October 17, 1973 when the Arab Kings and Sheikhs suddenly quadrupled the price of oil and threatened to cut off the supply. Since then oil has assumed the name, black gold (an expensive commodity). Its costliness is one of the main reasons for the economic crisis currently rocking the world from east to west to such an extent, that some countries, especially in third world, are strangled by debt.

backed by the Hadiths and writings of Islamic scholars, Muhammad took up the sword only when told to do so by Allah.

Sura 2:216; 4:73-80 leads us to believe that Muslims at first objected to the idea of engaging in physical combat to spread Islam. As a persecuted minority in Mecca, they understood Jihad to be a verbal defense of their faith. But the alluring benefit of material gains through plunder, the unrestricted use of female captives, and an automatic admittance into paradise proved too much of a temptation for the Muslims to resist. As a result, the initial expeditions could be better described as plundering exercises rather than "evangelistic" missions inspired by religious fervor.

In his new role as "Military General," Muhammad commanded a band of Islamic Jihadists to ambush a defenseless Meccan caravan and seize their goods. This took place in a month when all fighting was prohibited by treaty. When the Jihadists returned to Medina with their plunder, this unprovoked attack was unanimously condemned by the community. But what the people of Medina judged to be an armed robbery in broad daylight got divine approval:

"They ask thee concerning fighting in the prohibited month. Say: fighting therein is a grave [*offence*]: but graver is it in the sight of God to prevent access to the path of God to deny Him, to prevent access to the sacred mosque, and drive out its members. Tumult and oppression is worse than slaughter . . . " (Sura 2:217).

If you accept these statements as "revelations" from Allah, then you are faced with an Allah who admitted that fighting in the prohibited month was a "grave offence," but who turned around and defended the "grave offence" by saying that more "grave is preventing people from the sacred mosque". Two wrongs do not make a right nor do two sins make righteousness. The true God never defends sin. The conclusion that the promise of loot was one of the stimuli motivating Jihadists to fight can be plainly seen in the Koran. Listen to this sura:

"God promised you many gains that ye will acquire, and hath given you this in advance, and withheld men's hand from you, that it may be a token for the believers and that he may guide you to the right path" (Sura 48:20).

That the speaker made good his promise to enrich Jihadists with plunder is proven from the lives of Muslims who migrated to Medina with Muhammad. Many who came to Medina poverty-stricken left fortunes to their heirs.[1] With these earthly incentives and more in paradise, Islamic Jihad escalated until it became an all out war of subjugation, not only of individuals, but of whole nations and empires.

Philip Schaff, writing on the history of the Christian church, stated it this way:

> "The Sword", says Muhammad "is the key of heaven and hell; a drop of blood shed in the cause of Allah, a night spent in arms, is of more avail than two months of fasting and prayer; whoever falls in battle, his sins are forgiven, and at the day of judgment his limbs shall be supplied by the wings of angels and cherubim." This was the secret of his success. Idolaters had to choose between Islam, slavery and death; Jews and Christians were allowed to purchase a limited toleration by the payment of Jizya (humility tax), but were nonetheless kept in degrading bondage... The khalifs, Muhammad's successors who like him united the priestly and kingly divinity, carried on his conquests with the battle cry: "Before you is paradise, behind you are death and hell." Inspired by the weakness of the Byzantine empire and the internal distraction of the Greek church, the wild sons of the desert who were content with the plainest food, and disciplined in the school of war, hardship and recklessness of life, subdued Palestine, Syria and Egypt, embracing the classical soil of primitive Christianity. Thousands of Christian churches in the patriarchal diocese of Jerusalem, Antioch and Alexandria were ruthlessly destroyed or converted into mosques. Twenty years after Muhammad's death, the crescent ruled over a realm as large as the Roman Empire.

The command to fight for the cause of Allah is given in many Suras of the Koran:

> "Then fight in the cause of God and know that God heareth and knoweth all things" (Sura 2:244).

---

[1] Read of the life of Abd Rahman, in Rauzatu's Safa Vol. 2, P.253

The command to fight relentlessly is given in Sura 4:74. In Sura 8:65, Allah encouraged Muhammad to incite Muslims to fight. Listen to Allah giving the Jihad order:

> "But when the forbidden months are past, then fight and slay the pagans wherever ye find them, and seize them, beleaguer them and lie in wait (ambush) for them in every stratagem (of war) but if they repent, and establish regular prayers and practice regular charity, then open the way for them: for God is oft-forgiving most merciful" (Sura 9:5).

> "O ye who believe! fight the unbelievers . . . " (Sura 9:123).

Those who are ignorant of the Koran and Islam are terrified when they see Muslims slaughtering Christians, and rightly so. We might feel a little bit better about it if we understood that our Muslim friends are just doing what they believe to be right. Allah specifically commands Muslims to fight against Christians and Jews until they are reduced to a condition worst than that of slaves:

> "Fight those who believe not in God (*Allah*] and his apostle, nor acknowledge the religion of truth [*even if they are*] of the people of the book [*i.e. Jews and Christians*], until they pay jizya [*humiliating tax*] with willing submission, and feel themselves subdued [*enslaved*]" (Sura 9:29).

A being who is determined to wipe out Jews and Christians, now who might that be? The Bible has the answer:

> Rev 12:17 "And the dragon *(Satan)* was wroth with the woman *(Israel)*, and went to make war with the remnant of her seed *(the Jews today)*, which keep the commandments of God, and have the testimony of Jesus Christ *(the Christians)*."

Suppose you have two sons and one was stubborn. Would you instruct the good son to slay the stubborn? Of course not. No loving parent would do such a thing. If no earthly parent would do that, how much more would God not do so, the author of mercy. If the speaker in this sura is Allah (which I strongly believe him to be) then we have solid proof that Allah is totally different from the Bible God. The Bible God has a special love for

His people, the Jews and Christians. The Bible God warns against taking up Jihad against his people:

> "He suffered no man to do them wrong: yea, he reproved kings for their sakes; *Saying,* Touch not mine anointed, and do my prophets no harm." (Psa 105:14-15)

But in obedience to Allah's call to fight, Muhammad spent a great deal of his time between the Hijra (flight) and his death mapping out strategies for the purpose of spreading Islam, and personally getting involved in ambush attacks. Islamic historians themselves confirm that Muhammad was present at twenty six such armed conflicts and fought actively in nine (Risalatu Abdullah & C., 47, CF. Ibn Hisham Vol. 3, P. 78).

In thirteen years of ministry, Muhammad won just over a hundred souls to Islam by peaceful persuasions. But when he took up the sword "miracles" started to happen. People were forced to choose between Islam and violent death.[1] With death as the only option, eight years after the Hijra (flight), Muhammad could mobilize an army of about 10,000 Jihadists for his attack against Mecca (see Ibn Athir Vol.2, P. 93)

A year later, i.e. 9 A.H., 30,000 Jihadists attacked Tabuk. When Khalifah Abu Bakr captured Syria for Islam, the Islamic army had grown so large that the whole place was swarming with Jihadists.[2]

---

[1] Muhammad understood Jihad to mean literal war and even participated in those conflicts himself. As a result, moderate Muslims arguing against Jihad have no basis for their belief.

[2] Katib' Waqidi, Futuhu' Sham, Vol. 1, P. 6, Bombay edition, 1298 A.H.

Chapter 14

Islam & the Middle East Conflict

Contrary to what many believe, the origin of the Arab-Israeli conflict is neither the birth of the Jewish nation in 1948 nor the Palestinian issue. They appear to be real issues, but the conflict is really cultural and religious, and as such is spiritual – demonic and divine.

The root causes of the struggle can be traced back to Muhammad's time in Medina, about one thousand four hundred years ago.[1] When Muhammad arrived in Medina in 622 AD, there were three prominent Jewish communities, namely, Banu Qainuga, Banu Nadhir and Banu Quraizah. At first Muhammad tried to lure them into Islam by making some concessions to their religious customs, just the way he did for the pagans of Mecca. For instance, he commanded Muslims to turn their faces towards Jerusalem when praying. He even adopted the Jewish day of atonement and his "revelations" were favorably disposed towards them.

But Muhammad's attempts to win over the Jews proved abortive as they constantly exposed his ignorance of scripture, pointing out his deviations and distortions with bitter scorn. The Medinat suras that correspond to this period paint a vivid picture of Jewish accusations and Muhammad's counter accusations.

That the Jews slandered Muhammad and threatened to destroy his religious authority cannot be questioned. But this was not because Muhammad was an Arabian "prophet". They did the same to their own

---

[1]To a Westerner, this is quite a long time. But to an Easterner, it is like yesterday. Orientalists place a high premium on history. They draw historical parallels to events of thousands of years ago to prove a point. For instance, Saddam Hussein once called his war with Iran "Qadisiyyat Saddam", a reference to the Arab Jihad against Persia (Iran) fought nearly 1350 years ago.

and even to Jesus. They might even have told Muhammad that they would kill him the way they killed Jesus. A boast that Muhammad countered with sura 4:157.

In the face of this perceived Jewish threat, Muhammad first unleashed some "revelations" against them:

"Strongest among men in enmity to the believers (Muslims) will thou find the Jews and pagans . . ." (Sura 5:85).

Though they had previously been accorded the title of "ahl ul-kitab," meaning people of the book, the Jews of that book were now targeted for Jihad (sura 9:29).

Muhammad first moved against the Arabian Jews, apparently, in an effort to cleanse Arabia of Allah's enemies. He used various means, including pitting one Jewish clan against another and blockading their quarters until they surrendered (reminds one of the Nazi treatment of the Jews in the Warsaw ghetto, doesn't it.).

A month after the battle of Badr, Muhammad banished the Quinuga Jews to Jordan (Sura 59:14-15). Nadhir Jews were forced to relinquish their gold and weapons and then driven from their homes (Sura 59:1-7). The properties of the deportees were shared among Muslims.

After the battle of the ditch in 627AD, Muhammad at a market square commanded the surrendered Banu Quraiza Jews to dig trenches, then in the trenches they had just dug, he ordered that 700 male Jews of that clan be slaughtered, one after the other (Sura 33:26; cf. Ibn Hisham's Siratur Rasul, Part 2, pp. 75, 148). The "spared" widows, small children and properties were distributed among the "faithful" Muslims as their reward for helping Allah.

Poor Hitler! His great undoing was his failure to claim divine inspiration for his actions. If he had done so, we might even have another major religion in Europe – a Nazi version of Islam.

Muhammad himself chose the most beautiful among the widows, Rihanah bint Amr bin Khanafa. She however refused Muhammad's offer of marriage, preferring to be his concubine instead.

In a bid to avenge the massacre of her people, she served Muhammad a meal of goat meat poisoned with a fatal toxin that kills instantly. Bishr bin al-Bura, one of the companions of the prophet, died on the spot, right after swallowing a piece of the meat. Muhammad managed to spew out the one he was chewing, but traces of the toxin found its way into his system and caused a sickness that eventually led to his death.

It is related by Ibn Sa'ad that Muhammad sent for the Jewess and asked her, "Did you poison the ewe?" She said "Yes". He asked, "What made you do so?" She answered: "You had done to my people grievous damage. So I said that if you are a king, we will rid ourselves of you, and if you are a prophet, it will be revealed to you." Some historians claim he forgave her while others say he ordered her crucifixion.

That incident is the root cause of the virulent hatred the Muslims have towards the Jews. That is why Islam regards the Jews as the very worst enemy Allah has, and believes the Jews must be destroyed. Have you ever wondered why a non-Arabic nation like Iran is just as antagonistic towards Israel as the most radical Arab country? The story above is the answer. The Palestinian issue, the return of Arab's lands, all are just political window-dressing. The Palestinians have already been granted an autonomous state. The Sinai peninsula has already been returned to Egypt. Syria would have gotten back the Golan but for her intransigence. So why is there still no sign of peace? The truth is this: Muslims throughout the world do not believe the Jewish people should be allowed to exist. Even if the Jews were to totally abandon the Holy Land and be relocated elsewhere, that hatred would continue unabated and the conflict would go on (Revelation 12:17 figuratively foretells of this).

Faithful Muslims have been drumming Islam's militant agenda for decades, but we don't listen. Before Israel became a state, Ayatollah Khomeini was going into all the Islamic colleges, theological seminaries and schools in Iran, teaching them a five point program:

Stage 1: Iran must become a theocratic, fundamentalist Islamic State.

Stage 2: Iraq must become a theocratic, fundamentalist Islamic State.

Stage 3: Saudi Arabia, Jordan, Syria, Egypt, have to become fundamentalist and theocratic Islamic States.

Stage 4: Jerusalem must be retaken and the Jewish people destroyed.

Stage 5: Conquest of the nations.

As recent history shows, Stage 1 has been accomplished. There is no Muslim, fundamentalist or moderate, who does not believe in stages 4 and 5. Those five stages are bonds that unite all Muslims, regardless of sect or geographic location. Let's say it again, Islam's ambitions are:

(1) Annexation of Jerusalem and annihilation of the Jews
(2) Obliteration of Christianity
(3) Conquest of all nations.

To most Muslims, the failure to achieve these objectives means the failure of Islam and consequently, the failure of Allah – an unimaginable blasphemy. Islam will never renounce its claim to Jerusalem, neither will it relent in its effort to destroy the Jews. Consequently, the conflict in the Middle east is unsolvable. It is a war between Allah and "I AM" (see Zechariah 14:1-4).

In 1984, Ayatollah Khomeini declared to the entire world:

"In order to achieve the victory of Islam in the world, we need to provoke repeated crises, restored value to the idea of death and martyrdom. If Iran has to vanish, that is not important. The important thing is to engulf the world in crises. Those who are called to export the revolution will lose their unhealthy desire for comfort and will attain the maturity needed to fulfill their mission. The road to Jerusalem goes through Kerbala." (an Iraqi town)[1]

These are not the words of a naive, overwrought, emotional fanatic with stone-age ideas, as the West mistakenly concludes. Ayatollah Khomeini was one of the most politically brilliant theological minds in the Islamic world. He was able to perfectly express the mind of Allah and of Islam, and though he has been long dead, his manifesto lives on. I pray that United States political thinkers will heed what is written here, but their government is now so politically and morally bankrupt, that any departure from their policy of appeasing Islam is most unlikely. Blindly optimistic, the American bureaucracy totally ignores the Muslim view of any treaty signed with infidels.[2]

Muhammad himself, never honored a peace treaty, an example being his Nakhla expedition – a banditry operation he ordered during a month of general truce. Another example was his attack on Mecca despite

---

[1] Quoted in *Le Point, No. 599*, March 12, 1984, pp. 89-90

[2] Editor's Note: Hillary Clinton, the American president's wife, in a 3/22/99 speech delivered in Egypt, declared that the United States would be more accepting of Islam in the future. Insanity! If Islam ever gains political control in the United States, religious tolerance will be a thing of the past anywhere in the world.

the treaty of al-Hudaybiya. This spirit of non-committal to peace treaties is an integral part of Jihad. Muhammad once said that Jihad means trickery. The count-down to the battle of Armageddon will begin the day Israel signs its death treaty with her Arab neighbors (what they think to be a peace treaty will actually be a death warrant for Israel). Not that one is against peace, but why sign a treaty with those whose intent is to destroy you? It is ludicrous to believe that the Arabs will sacrifice Allah's cause with Allah's worst enemies. Hstege fu-lai-llah, – Allah forbid. Such a treaty would only be a ploy, designed to trick Israel into lowering its guard, and thus opening the way for a blitzkreig attack. The type they launched October 17, 1973 during Yom-Kippur. Rest assured, the Arabs will attack Israel again when they believe they can defeat her.

But how sure are we that the countdown has not begun? Islam has even gained a foothold in the Knesset (Israeli Parliament). In the Israeli election that brought Benjamin Netanyahu to power, a Muslim won a parliamentary seat. As a result, a provision for a mosque has been made in the Knesset, where the name of Allah – a being who wants them annihilated – will be invoked daily. A catastrophic occurrence indeed, and an abomination in the eyes of "I AM!"

The Western nations have compounded the problem by ignoring the irreconcilable spiritual differences that exist between themselves and the Muslim states. The Muslim goal first, last, and always has been to Islamize the world by the power of the sword. But despite the obvious threat to themselves, the West is only worried about its balance of payments – imports and exports. Money is their god. That attitude has permitted the West to sell nuclear technology to the Arabs – nuclear pigeons that will eventually fly home to roost in the nose-cones of Islamic rockets.[1] It is an accepted fact that only a year or so separates Iraq and Iran from weapons of mass destruction. It won't be long before the Jihad we live with in Nigeria reaches its bloody sword across the Atlantic, and the West suffers for its diplomatic hypocrisy.

---

[1] Editor's Note: The wealthy Arabian terrorist, Osama bin Laden, has stated publically that he would explode two nuclear devices in the United States in the year 2000 as his part in the ever-expanding Islamic Jihad against the West. Whether or not bin Laden can make good on his threat remains to be seen, but that he is at war with the West is patently obvious. US intelligence agencies have already implicated Bin Laden in two US embassy bombings.

Chapter 15

Christians,
the Birth of Islam
& Jihad

As earlier noted, a time came when Islam was so persecuted that eighty-three Muslims had to flee for safety to Abyssinia, a Christian country (now Ethiopia). The Negus and his Christian subjects protected the Muslims and lavished love on them. When the Meccan persecutors demanded their repatriation, the Christians refused to hand them over. The Muslims had earlier defended their faith in public debate, confessing their belief in Christ's Virgin birth, His miracles, and His ascension into heaven (the favorable passages about Jesus in the Koran may have been "revealed" for that purpose). If those refugees were not outright willful deceivers, one wonders why they did not state their position on Christ's sonship, His death on the cross, and subsequent resurrection?

In any case, Muhammad's accommodation with the Christians was short-lived. After Islam became fully established, it revealed its true color as a rabid anti-Christian religion, and the blotting out of Christianity from under heaven has been a major aim of Islam ever since. In their quest to destroy Christianity, Muslims even went as far as to forge a false "gospel," allegedly written by Barnabas.[1]

Following in the footsteps of their prophet, Muhammad's successors, the Khalifahs, launched a Jihad against Christendom – in Mesopotamia, Asia minor, central Asia, and in Egypt – killing millions and forcing the rest to embrace Islam.[2] Then they attacked and occupied Jerusalem. As if

---

[1] Barnabas is believed to have been written by a monk named Marino, a Catholic turned Muslim, who was later known as Mustapha Arandi. Barnabas contains direct quotes from the Koran and from a 15th century comedy by Dante.

[2] Before his death in 632, Muhammad ordered a military operation against Christian Byzantine (the Eastern Roman Empire).

all this wasn't enough, on the very site where the magnificent temple of the "I AM" once stood, the Muslims chose to construct the Dome of the Rock and their third most "holy" mosque (the mosque of Omar). Why was the Dome placed where it was, if not to desecrate the temple site of the Bible God?[1]

The Muslims undid most of the achievements of the early apostles by invading Christian populated North Africa, slaughtering many, and forcing the rest to Islam at the point of the sword. Even today it is a crime to preach Christ in most of the Middle Eastern countries. For instance, in Arabia, if a Saudi national is found to be a Christian, he is beheaded.

The battle-hardened Islamic "missionaries" swept over Palestine, drove on to Persia, continued their drive into northwest India, and settled finally on the southern steps of Russia. They overran Spain and invaded France. Thank God for Charles Martel who halted their advance into Europe. But for that battle, Islam could have overrun the whole continent. Sadly enough, Islam is now using their petrol dollars to achieve what they could not accomplish earlier through the sword. Through its control of oil, Islam is now expanding at the expense of the Christian world. [2]

---

[1] Editor's Note: The exact location of God's temple was unknown to the Muslim builders of the Dome of the Rock so they missed desecrating the temple by 300 ft. The dome is actually located in what was once known as "the court of the Gentiles." Jerry Landay in his book, *The Dome of the Rock* (Newsweek, New York, NY, 1972) p. 18, records that when Khalifah Omar entered Jerusalem in 639AD, he was met by Sophronius, Bishop of the Jerusalem Church, who showed him through the city. Looking at the temple mount (then in rubble), Omar declared that he was going to build a memorial to Muhammad on the original site of the temple of God. Sophronius exclaimed in horror, "Verily, this is the Abomination of Desolation spoken of by Daniel the prophet, and it now stands in the holy place," (Daniel 9:27) Though Sophronius was an old man of about 80, Khalifah Omar put him in prison and to forced manual labor, the rigors of which killed him. A new understanding of biblical day=years has proved Sophronius' utterance to be both prophetic and true. See Ellis Skolfield, *Sozo, Survival Guide for a Remnant Church* (Fish House Publishing, Fort Myers, FL, 1995).

[2] Editor's Note: This second spread of Islam was foretold in great detail in the Bible book of Revelation. See Ellis Skolfield, *Sozo, Survival Guide for a Remnant Church* (Fish House Publishing, Fort Myers, FL, 1995).

Important dates in the Islamic conquest:

632 AD – Islamic Jihadists conquered Yemen.

632 AD – Invasion of Abyssinia (Ethiopia) but the invading Islamic army was repelled by the orthodox church backed by the Portugese. This was a particularly disgraceful event, because just seventeen years earlier, Abyssinia had helped the persecuted Muslims.

633 AD – All the desert tribes of Arabia were thoroughly subdued through military campaigns.

635 AD – The attacking Islamic army burst through the Euphrates river (Iraq) and conquered Damascus.

637 AD – The Persians (Iranians) were defeated at the battle of Qadisiyya.

637 AD – The fall of Iraq

638 AD – Islamic fighters occupied Jerusalem.

639 AD – All of Syria fell into Muslims hands.

642 AD – All of Egypt fell to Muslims after some resistance in Alexandria. The great Coptic church was destroyed never to know strength again.

670 AD – Khalif Muawiya ordered an unsuccessful sea assault against Byzantium.

688 AD – The fall of Carthage.

702 AD – The Berber tribes of North Africa conquered.

705 - 708 AD – Occupation of North Africa.

711-713 AD – Arabian expansionists captured all of Spain and Portugal. The place the Islamic Commander pitched his headquarters still bears his name, Gibralter, in English, or Jebel Tariq (Arabic), meaning mountain of Tariq.

715-717 AD – Arabian armies subdued Afghanistan, central Asia, northern limit of the Caspian sea, much of northern India.

718 AD – Islamic forces started attacking France.

725 AD – The invading Islamic armies besieged Toulouse and raided Burgundy and the Rhone valley.

732 AD – Bordeaux was besieged. The Islamic armies advanced up to Poitiers where they were defeated by Charles Martel.

And thus, just one century after the death of Muhammad, the domain of Islam stretched from the Pyrenees to the Himalayas, from the Atlantic to the Indian Ocean, and from central Asia to central Africa.

From 750 AD onwards, Islam went through a period of stagnation. For a time, intellectual, commercial and artistic pursuit became more prominent, and by the eleventh century, the Islamic empire was weak enough for the Vatican to venture the crusades. However, this provoked the Muslims to more conquests:

11th Century AD – Muslims penetrated Africa south of the Sahara.

11th - 14th Century AD – Muslims' occupation of northern India.

13th Century AD – A band of Muslim states linked Dakar (Senegal) to the Red Sea across the sub-Sahara prairies.

14th - 16th Century AD – Muslim fighters conquered Indonesia.

15th Century AD – Constantinople fell. That city (renamed Istanbul) was the eastern bastion of the whole of the Christian world. The great Christian church of Santa Sofia built by Christian emperor Justinian, was turned into a mosque.

1804 AD – Islamic Jihadists conquered northern Nigeria.

Islam (A Brief Historical Background)

Since many western nations have a distorted or vague knowledge of Islam, it is essential to give a brief historical background of this political entity that is also a religion.

Islam literally means submission. Consequently a true Muslim is one who submits. Islam is not Muhammadanism nor are Muslims Muhammadans. Such terms are a misnomer and offensive to Muslims. Islam revolves around a central figure called Muhammad, but that does not mean the religion is built around or on Muhammad. According to Muslims he was only an instrument of Allah.

Muhammad was born in 570 AD in Mecca (correctly pronounced Makka), a city northwest of Arabia. His father, Abdullah (meaning servant of Allah) died before he was born. His mother, Amina, died when he was six. He was raised, first by his grandfather, Abdul Muttalib, and later by his uncle, Abdul Manaf, also known as Abu Talib. He was of the Hashimite clan of Quraish tribe. As a young boy he traveled with his uncle in merchant caravans to Syria, and for some years after he made similar journeys in the service of a wealthy widow named Khadija. Muhammad is said to have so faithfully transacted the widow's business that she, at age forty, married Muhammad who was then twenty-five. This marriage made Muhammad quite influential, as his wife's vast wealth was now at his disposal. It should be noted that as long as Khadija lived, Muhammad was a strict monogamist (their marriage lasted 25 years).

Muhammad was a man of markedly religious disposition whose dissatisfaction with the paganism and crude superstitions of his native Mecca made him join a group who claimed they were in search of the religion of Abraham. They were known as hunafa (sing. Hanif)). It was his habit to retire for a month of every year to a cave in the desert for meditation. His locale of retreat was Hira, a desert hill about 3 miles north of Mecca, and the month he chose for his meditation was Ramadan. It was in the course of such meditation that he heard a voice say: "Iqraa!", meaning "recite!". The command was twice repeated, and Muhammad asked what he was to recite. The voice replied, "Recite thou in the name of the Lord who created man from a clot of blood". (Sura 96). It should be noted from the onset, that the spirit that inspired Muhammad was a spirit of error, for man was not created from a clot of blood, but from the dust of the ground (Genesis 2:7). At first, Muhammad was not sure of the source of the revelations, was it from the jinn, the creatures who inspired the soothsayers? Or was it from God? He shared his worries with his wife (Khadija) who gave him much encouragement.

A renowned Islamic historian, Imam At-Tabari relates this incident in his book entitled "Tarik ar-Rasul wa'l Muluk":

> "Then (Gabriel) departed from me, and I went off making my way back to my family. I went straight to Khadija and seated myself on her thigh to seek refuge there. She said, "...What is it, O son of my uncle? Could it be you have seen something?" "Yes, I answered and then related to her what I have seen. She replied, "Rejoice, O son of my uncle, and hold fast. By Him in whose hand is Khadija's soul, I hope that you are to be the prophet of this people."

Khadija did not leave Muhammad with her counsel alone. She consulted her cousin, too, who happens to be one of the hunafa:

> "Then she arose...and went off to Waraqa ibn Naufal, who was her cousin on the paternal side. This Waraqa had become a Christian, had read the scriptures and had listened to the people of the Law (Torah), and the Gospel (Injil). To him she set forth what the apostle of God had told her. Said Waraqa, 'Qudus! Qudus! By Him in whose hand is Waraqa's soul, if you are telling the truth, O Khadija, there has indeed come the great Namua;' and by Namua he meant Gabriel who used to come to Moses. 'So

he will assuredly be the prophet of his people.' So Khadija returned to Muhammad and informed him of what Waraqa had said and that eased the anxiety he had felt."

After the incident related above, Muhammad himself met Waraqa at the shrine of Ka'aba and related his experience again:

"Thereupon Waraqa said, 'By Him in whose hand is my soul, thou are assuredly to be the prophet of this people, for there has indeed come unto thee the great Namus that came to Moses,' ...And the apostle of Allah went to his house, encouraged by the word of Waraqa, so that some of the anxiety he felt was relieved". (Leiden edition. Pp. 147-152).

You can see this confirmed in commentary No. 31 & 32 of the Koran translated by Abdullah Yusuf Ali, a translation honored by all Muslims.

The counseling and encouragement of Khadija and Waraqa were instrumental in establishing Muhammad as a prophet. Before anyone remarks on the roles of Khadija and Waraqa, one needs to know the religious setting in pre-Islamic Arabia. The Jews and Christians were said to be priding themselves (because of their scriptures) over the Arabs who had no scripture (cf. Ahmed Deedat, Christ in Islam, p. 32). This made the Arabs feel inferior; so it is not surprising that Muhammad was encouraged. Now the Arabs would have their own prophet and scripture, and the boasting of Christians and Jews would be silenced.

Some western authors dispute the fact that Muhammad was given revelations from a spirit entity. That ignores the spiritual dimension. Muhammad did indeed receive "revelations," over a span of 22 years. What remains suspect is the identity of the "angel" who whispered in his ear. I have heard some people exclaim, "Oh! If only someone could have met Muhammad and given him the truth!" But the hard truth is: Muhammad or no Muhammad, some kind of false religion would come to Arabia – a prophet and an Islam or something similar. Genesis chapter sixteen verses eleven and twelve still had to be fulfilled . . .

Gen 16:11 (KJV) "And the angel of the LORD said unto her, Behold, thou *art* with child, and shalt bear a son, and shalt call his name Ishmael; because the LORD hath heard thy affliction."

Gen 16:12 (KJV) "And he will be a wild man; his hand *will be* against every man, and every man's hand against him; and he shall dwell in the presence of all his brethren."

And eventually, a Middle Eastern Islam did raise its hand against every man and every man's hand was against it.

When Muhammad made the claim that he was the apostle of Allah, his household believed him at once. That included Khadija, his wife, Ali, his cousin and Zaid ibn Haritha – a freed slave and Muhammad's adopted son. The first convert outside his family was a rich and honorable merchant called Abu Bakr.

At the age of forty-three, Muhammad went to the public square around Ka'aba to preach. He proclaimed that Allah was one, unseen and all-powerful. He condemned the worship of other gods beside Allah and warned of a coming day of judgment. In thirteen years of peaceful preaching, he won about a hundred souls. As previously stated, persecution broke out and some of his followers fled to Abyssinia (now Ethiopia, a Christian country).

Since Islam is not just a religious but a political entity, and since politics is a game of compromise, Muhammad made concessions to his Arabian opponents by recognizing and worshiping their idols (Al-Lat, Al-Uzza and Manat) (Sura 53:18-22). When these concessions backfired, Muhammad blamed Satan for fixing the "revelations" in his mouth (Sura 22:52). It is interesting to note that these satanic verses came in the same way as his earlier "revelations," but still, Muhammad did not suspect that all might have had the same source.

June 25th, 622 AD marked the turning point in Islam as Muhammad migrated (Hijra) to Yatrib (now Medina) and was declared as head of state and commander in chief of the first Islamic Umma (community of believers). Muslims start their dating from that year. Thus, according to Islam, we are in the fifteenth century not the twentieth. That anti-Christ would attempt to change time and seasons is stated in black and white in Daniel 7:25:

"He will speak against the most high and oppress his saints and try to change the set time and laws . . ." (NIV)

Once Muhammad had consolidated his position in Medina, Allah commanded him to wage a Jihad. Attacks and counter attacks continued until a ten year peace pact was signed with the Meccans, known as the treaty of Al-Hudaybiyah. This treaty was just a ploy, and Muhammad invaded Mecca two years later with ten thousand Jihadists (cf. Daniel 11:23-24). Knowing that resistance would be suicidal, the Meccans surrendered unconditionally.

Muhammad's bitter enemies, Abu Sufyan, Suhail and the like, saved their lives by immediately switching over to Islam. Those who could not do so were summarily executed (Another sterling example of Allah's tender "mercy"). Since then, Islam has maintained a steady expansion, much of it by open military aggression. Maybe that's where Mao Tse Tung got the idea that power flows through the barrel of a gun.

Chapter 16

The Nigerian Experience

Our own country of Nigeria has not been spared the Islamic sword. Uthman Dan Fodio launched a Jihad on this country in the 19th century. Since then, the Christians have been continually living at the mercy of their Muslim neighbors. We need not go to the historical archives to find out what Jihad is like. In obedience to Allah's injunction, Muslims regularly slaughter Christians here, and at random. It is not within the scope of this book to chronicle all the bloodshed that has taken place in Nigeria, but here are a few examples:

In the North, with the full backing of local authorities, Churches are pulled down at will. The excuse? The North is an Islamic State. The author was in Kano in 1980, when an Islamic Maitatsine riot broke out there, killing 4,177 people (official figure) with millions of Naira worth of properties destroyed. In October 1982, the Islamic faithful were again destructive, setting eight big churches ablaze. In that same year, the Muslims in Kaduna went berserk, slaying 400 people (official figure).

In 1984, the Islamic volcano erupted in Yola and Jimeta, killing 700 people, including some policemen, and rendered 5,913 people homeless. In March 1987, Muslims in Kaduna, Zaria, Kafanchan and Katsina launched a half-week Jihad against Christians. In Zaria alone, all one hundred big churches were fire-bombed. Several Christians were butchered and many others were roasted to death. Many known Christian buildings were destroyed. In all those cities, any motor vehicle that displayed a Christian sticker was attacked.

In April 1991, Muslims in Bauchi went on an indiscriminate killing spree, burning down churches and destroying a great deal of personal property. About 350 people were killed.

Almost simultaneously, Katsina was troubled. Ibrahim Zakari alias El-Zakzaki invaded the city with over 2,000 Shi'ite Muslim fundamentalists to help Yakubu Yahaya (his devout student) in a running battle with Colonel John Madaki, the State Governor. Lives were lost and property was destroyed.

On October 14th 1991, the Muslims in Kano went on rampage again, ostensibly to disrupt a crusade during which the German-born evangelist, Reinhard Bonnke, was to preach. They planned to murder Bonnke himself. It is difficult to arrive at the exact casualty figure there, because many of the murdered Christians were dumped in wells. However, it is estimated that over 2,000 Christians were cut down by the Islamic sword. In this case, however, the Muslims, too, suffered casualties. I quote a few lines from page 16 of the Oct. 28, 1991 edition of *Newswatch* magazine:

> "But unlike in previous religious riots in which non-indigenes (*people not native to the area*) and Christians turned the other cheek or ran for their lives, this time they hit back. Within hours of the fundamentalists unleashing a reign of terror, the non-indigenes mobilized themselves into a militia force, brandishing cutlasses, matchets, iron rods and broken bottles in a counter attack."

The Lord Jesus not only told us to turn the other cheek, but to do so until slapped 70 x 7 times. As this incident in Kano illustrates, Christians may have reached that 70 x 7 limit. We have suffered 1,400 years of relentless assault by Muslims. Our centuries of non-resistance were not weakness, as they wrongly imagined, but in obedience to the Bible.

In May 1992, Zangon-Kataf, a town about 200 km south of Kaduna was destroyed, the Muslim settlers clashing with the indigenous church-going Kataf. The entire town was devastated and farmlands destroyed. The destruction was so total that federal authorities embarked on reconstruction and rehabilitation.

Within a few days, the war spread to Kaduna. The Muslim plan was to attack Christians during their Sunday worship services. They struck at 8 PM, local time, slaughtering people from house to house, chanting "Allahu Akbar" as they went. Many churches were set ablaze, and as usual, other Christian buildings were targeted. Thousands perished.

If Christians are eliminated who will then preach the Gospel to them, reason the Muslims. But many Christians in Kaduna didn't want to be slaughtered like chickens anymore. In this crisis Muslims learned that mosques burn as easily as a church, and that Muslims can die as quickly as Christians. War is an ill wind that blows no one any good!

On September 14, 1994, the Islamic faithfuls struck Potiskum, Yobe State (North East Nigeria), killing three people including an ECWA church Pastor, Yahaya Tsalibi, who was conducting communion service. Nine churches were set ablaze and 15,000,000 Naira worth of property was destroyed (Police estimate).

In Kano, on December 26, 1994, Mr. Gideon Akaluka (a Christian) was openly beheaded by a mob of Muslim faithful for allegedly defiling a portion of the Koran. They paraded around the city with his severed head, chanting a victory slogan.

In Sokoto, northwest Nigeria, another Christian was mercilessly beaten because a Muslim beggar who asked of alms accused him of insulting the prophet Muhammad. Mr. Azubuike was more fortunate than most; he was thought dead and abandoned.

July 1-7, 1995, Muslims attacked Sayawa Christian community of Tafawa Balewa, Local Govt. Area, Bauchi State (northeast Nigeria). The Muslim's first port of call was the Tafawa Balewa central market, which they set ablaze. They burned down the home of the late Mr. Bukata Adamu who had lost the rest of his family to a similar riot in 1991. The Muslims then proceeded to attack and burn down 30 Sayawa Christian villages. Over 1,000 homes were razed in this inferno. Christians were killed by the thousands. Seventy-seven churches were burnt to the ground. Properties worth millions of Naira were destroyed. Not even women and children were spared in this genocidal Jihad – the Islamic faithful slaughtering 36 women and children who had taken refuge at a church building in a village named Gungu-Zango. The women even had their bellies ripped open. In a village called Bununu, in Bula district, which is not inhabited by the Sayawas, twenty-two school children (ages 11 to 16 years) were trapped and butchered by Muslims.

Wouldn't you think the police or military would come to the rescue of these defenseless people? Not a chance, and no Muslim ever stood before a court of law to answer for the numerous acts of vandalism, not to mention the countless murders they committed in Bauchi State. Instead, Sayawa Christians, the victims of that Jihad, had to stand trial before a military tribunal for causing of the trouble. A gross miscarriage of justice, certainly, but eventually one becomes accustomed to the ever-present threat of governmental injustice or Muslim violence. So accustomed to it, in fact, that we just call it the "Nigerian Factor."

The religious fervor that caused above atrocities is not going to go away. Those Nigerian authorities who think they can appease Muslims by supporting them against the Christians need a better understanding of Islamic law. According to the Koran, true Muslims cannot be appeased until a pure (non-negotiable) Islamic government with a Sharia (fundamental Islamic) constitution is in force. [1]

Even worse than the atrocities is the apathy of the church towards Muslim evangelism, for the problem lies not with a people who are worse than any other. It lies in the religious system they have been taught and so earnestly believe. As long as Muslims believe the Koran to be of God, they will continue to burn, rape, and murder its opponents.

But the established churches, little realizing they dance to the enemy's tune, are not concerned about the salvation of Muslims, neither do they encourage any ministry that has a vision to reach them. The church in northern Nigeria is seen as a stranger's fellowship – the native-born people viewing Christianity as an alien religion brought in by foreigners. Even the few Muslims that from time to time do come to Christ are not properly discipled, which sends most of them back into Islam.

A current spiritual plague, the "name it and claim it theology," has aggravated the situation, as people become "Christians" for an unbiblical, but much preached about material blessing. What ever happened to the true Gospel? That we come to Jesus because we need to know the Savior who came to earth, not as a conquering king, but to die. The Jesus who deliberately sacrificed His life to save us from all our sins.

---

[1] Editor's Note: That's not just Nigerian authorities, but governments everywhere who try to reach a diplomatic accord with the Muslim states or the Palestinians. By true Islamic law, it is not only permissible but laudable to lie, cheat, steal and even murder anyone who is not a Muslim. Islamic militants will not depart from their stated intent of destroying Israel and the United States just because of some worthless paper they signed but have no intention of honoring. The liberal media in the West blindly applauds such agreements as wonderful new "peace initiatives," but the western nations will eventually pay a staggering price for failing to understand and defend themselves against a militant Islam.

Chapter 17

Jihad &
Modern Muslims

Modern civilization actually works against Islam. Jihad that was enthusiastically employed as a means of propagating Islam during the dark ages is now an embarrassment to many moderate Muslims. Some try to explain away the high level of terrorism perpetrated by various radical Islamic groups, but all recognize Jihad as part of today's reality.

While writing this book, I was deeply touched by a newspaper account of a speech given by Egyptian President, Hosni Mubarak. I quote from that article:

"Egyptian President Hosni Mubarak, in his most open attack on Muslim fundamentalism has denounced people who use religious extremism and intellectual terrorism for 'cheap political gains.' They are not even alarmed when their illicit trade tarnish the image of Muslims and weakens the status of the Muslim nations before the world. 'This flagrant negativism is an illness which must be confronted courageously,' Mubarak said.

"A political analyst close to Mubarak commented: 'This is the first time the president tackles the phenomena of fundamentalism with total courage. Instead of denying and hiding, Mubarak took the straight forward approach.'

"Mubarak who saw his predecessor, Anwar Sadat, shot dead by Muslim extremists as he sat next to him at a military parade in 1981 declared: 'We must distance ourselves from sectarian divisions, reject religious extremism, fight intellectual terrorism and defend our nation from religious abuse.' He called for religious tolerance including allowing non-Muslims to practice their faith freely in Muslim states.

"Mubarak denounced the repeated use of violence by extremists against police and innocent bystanders. Backing most of the speech with verses of the Koran, Mubarak said Islam stressed freedom of belief. 'Conviction is never achieved by violence and (Islam) does not enter the mind or the heart by the sword,' he declared."[1]

Less than two weeks after Mubarak's speech, on April 15th 1992, the U.N. Security Council imposed an air travel and arms embargo on Libya. This action was taken because Libya refused to hand over the two men who were implicated in the blowing up of the Pan-Am passenger plane over Lockerbie, Scotland, a 1988 terrorist act in which 270 innocent people were killed.[2] That month was certainly eventful. In it, the Islamic Salvation Front of Algeria asked its members to take up arms against the government and the radical Muslims in Afghanistan captured Kabul.

The Iranian sponsored Hizbollah (Party of Allah) continually bombards northern Israel with all sorts of offensive weapons: rocket-propelled grenades, artillery pieces and self-propelled howitzers, and sets ambushes and booby traps for Israeli soldiers.

With inflammatory Jihad rhetoric flowing from the lips of the late Ayatollah Khomeini, thousands of youths volunteered for the Iran/Iraq war even when it was confirmed that the Iraqis were using highly toxic chemical weapons and lethal napalm bombs.

On Tuesday 5th and Friday 8th May 1992, Radio France International reported the death of fifty people as Islamic fundamentalists attacked Coptic Christians in Egypt, and attacks against them continue.

If the Koran is to be believed, and Muhammad is the model of correct Islamic behavior, these so called "extremists" or "fundamentalists" are the true Muslims. The Muslims who are hungry for Christian flesh and thirsty for their blood are really the ones who are obeying what Allah says:

"Therefore when ye meet the unbelievers [*in fight*] smite at their necks; at length, when ye have thoroughly subdued them, bind a bond firmly [*on them*]" (Sura 47:4).

---

[1] The speech he made to mark Leilat Al-Kadr, as it appeared on Page 5 of *Nigeria Daily Times*, April 2nd 1992.

[2] Editor's Note: To date, Libya has still refused to allow those men to be extradited to stand trial. Here is why. Fundamental Muslims do not see those men as murderers, but as warriors in Jihad. True Muslims are fighting an all-out war against the West, a war that the West is too blinded by its dependance on Arab oil to see.

"True Muslims" will ever wish unbelievers (especially Jews and Christians) dead as long as this kind of inciting Suras remain in the Koran. Islam has divided the world into two distinct camps: Dar al-Islam, i.e. the household of Islam, and Dar al-Harb, i.e. the household of war. Everyone who is not a Muslim is in Dar al-Harb. They are regarded as enemies of Allah whose heads must be chopped off.

There are verified reports that some Islamic countries are developing nuclear weapons. All peace-loving people of the world should be on their knees praying against this, because if the Muslim nations succeed, as sure as night follows day they will use those weapons in Jihad. The same is true of the biological and chemical weapons they are developing.

As previously discussed, many still argue that Allah is just the Arabic name for the true God. They obviously don't know the origin of Islam. Fine and convincing as their arguments may sound, Jesus warned sternly that we should not be carried away by every wind of doctrine, but rather that we should judge such men by their fruits. For He says:

"By their fruits we shall know them" (Matthew 7:15, 16).

Paraphrasing the verse, Jesus is saying: what you claim or say does not matter near as much as what your character is or how you behave.

What of the Wars in the Bible?

The wars the Israelites fought were purely national or political wars that they are still fighting to this day. These were not religious wars initiated to propagate their faith. The Bible God knows that forcing people to embrace a religion amounts to making hypocrites of them.

What about the Crusades?

The Crusades cannot be said to be truly Christian since nowhere did Jesus command his followers to fight for or take Jerusalem.[1] Our Lord Jesus

---

[1] Editor's Note: With the new understanding of Revelation available to the Church since 1967, it is now apparent that the first horn of the "beast with two horns," (Rev 13:11) was the Crusades. They "spake as a dragon," i.e., the Crusaders were influenced by Satan. History documents the many terrible atrocities that were committed by Crusaders against the local inhabitants in the Holy Land.

Christ, being the Prince of Peace, was always going about doing good, and healing all that were oppressed by the devil (Acts 10:38).

- He heals multitude of people (Mark 1:32-34).
- He cleanses lepers of leprosy (Matthew 8:2-3).
- He restores paralyzed men (Matthew 9:6).
- He manufactures eyes for men born blind (John 9:1-7).
- He feeds thousands by a miracle (Matthew 14:16-21).
- He brings the dead back to life (John 11:37-44) etc.

Jesus is not just a physical healer, he is also a spiritual healer. His blood is the only cure for our sin sicknesses.

How did Jesus treat His opponents?

Jesus not only taught that we should love our enemies but also practiced it. In one of his preaching trips, the Samaritans refused him passage through their territory (his miracles notwithstanding). His disciples got so angry that they wanted to bring fire down from Heaven upon them, but Jesus said:

"Ye know not what manner of spirit ye are of. For the Son of Man [*Jesus*] is not come to destroy men's lives but to save them" (Luke 9:51-56).

Jesus knew who was to betray Him, but He did not curse. When Jesus was arrested and later crucified He dissuaded Peter from defending Him with the sword, saying:

"Put up again thy sword into its place: for all they that take the sword shall perish with the sword" (Matthew 26:52).

Mr. murderer, do you hear that? They that take the sword shall perish by the sword, says Jesus. He even prayed for those that nailed Him to the cross saying:

"Father forgive them for they know not what they do" (Luke 24:34).

Can you imagine a person using his last breath to pray for his killers? Not only Jesus, but many Christian martyrs have done just that, ever since Jesus died. Can any person in his right mind put Jesus and Muhammad on the same pedestal? What concord hath Christ with Belial?

". . . because Christ also suffered for us leaving us an example, that ye should follow his steps: who did no sin, neither was guile found in his mouth: who, when he was reviled, reviled not again; when he suffered he threatened not" (1 Peter 2:21-23).

Even though our Muslim friends are commanded by Allah to kill us, we must respond with Christ's command that we love our enemies and pray for our persecutors (Matthew 5:44).

"For the love of Christ constraineth us" (2 Corinth. 5:14).

There are countless supernatural beings who claim to be God. But Allah included, they all fall short of the kind, loving and forgiving nature of the true God of the Bible. Listen to what He says:

"Whosoever hateth his brother is a murderer: and ye know that no murderer hath eternal life abiding in him. Hereby perceive we the love *of God*, because he laid down his life for us: and we ought to lay down *our* lives for the brethren" (1 John 3:15-16)

Chapter 18

Aljana, the Islamic Version of Heaven

Just as Muslims have their own god – Allah – they also have their own heaven – Aljana. As the Muslim Allah is totally different from the Christian God, so also is Aljana completely different from the biblical heaven. Not only is the method of entry into the two different, but the conditions there are markedly different.

In Sura 5:92; 2:219, Allah forbids Muslims from taking wine while on planet earth, but those going to Aljana are promised rivers of wine of many enticing varieties (Sura 47:15; 76:6):

- There is the promise of pure sealed wine (Sura 83:25)
- Zanjabil enhanced wine (Sura 76:17)
- Tasnim brand of wine (Sura 83:27)
- Wine mixed with kafur (Sura 76:5)

The Bible explicitly teaches that drunkards will not enter the Kingdom of God (1 Corinthians 6:9-10).

Recognizing the inherent weakness in their concept of heaven, Islamic scholars such as Muhiyyu'ddin endeavored to explain the wine away in a mystical sense, but he was called as a heretic by other Muslims who insisted that the Koran means exactly what it says. Yusuf Ali also tried to give the wine Suras sufic, i.e., spiritual renderings. But the frequency with which those references occurred and the unequivocal nature of them made him abandon the "sufic interpretation project" and toe the line of the generality of the Islamic umma – that the Koran means exactly what it says – real wine.

If they guzzle all that promised wine, I wonder if the Muslims will go berserk in Aljana just like they do here? You can't rule out that possibility, you know, since even without wine, they went berserk in Allah's headquarters (the Ka'aba in Mecca) during the pilgrimage of August 1987.

According to an official report by the Saudis, 402 Muslims were killed and 605 injured in a Jihad that they waged against themselves. Can their saying "Islam is peace" be true? Surely, a change of environment does not mean a change of heart. How the various warring factions of Islam can dwell together in the same Aljana is not stated by the Koran. Allah may have taken notice of this and compartmentalized the place. It appears that the Islamic Aljana contains what the Arabian desert most lacks, such as:

- Gushing water (Sura 3:15, 198, 4:57, 15:48).
- Clustered plantains (Sura 56:29)
- Fruits (Sura 56:20, 69:21-24).
- Shades with bunches of fruits (Sura 76:14).
- Enclosed gardens and grape vines (Sura 78:32).
- Fowl meat is one more carrot that Allah dangles before the noses of the Muslim faithful. (Sura 56:2).

Whereas the Bible says:

"For the Kingdom of God is not meat and drink; but righteousness, and peace, and joy in the Holy Ghost" (Romans 14:17).

Apart from the wine and such other worldly things, there is also supposed to be a lot of honeymooning in Aljana. Womanizing Muslims here on earth are a picture of morality compared to what supposedly awaits them in their heaven. Among the rewards promised faithful Muslims are beautiful and heavy women with big and lustrous eyes (Sura 38:52; 44:54; 52:20). (Whether this is where the idea of Ikebe Super[1] originates or not, I cannot tell). Also promised are virgins whom no jinn (demon) nor man has ever touched (Sura 55:70-74).

Hadiths by respected scholars confirm all this by telling us that each faithful Muslim will be entitled to several thousand of these "special" women, called Houris (cf. Mishkatu'l Masabih, pp. 457-491). This concept of heaven contradicts the words of our Lord Jesus who dismissed a similar but more restrained sensual notion of the Sadducees. Jesus told

---

[1] "Ikebe Supers" are imaginary ladies of comic strip proportions with mountainous buttocks and the kind of breasts as described in the Koran.

them plainly that there would be no marriage in heaven (See Matthew 22:29, 30).

What will happen to Muslim women from this world? Who would marry them considering that Muslim men are offered a whole host of better "heavenly" virgins? Would you go for a slightly used model when you were offered thousands of brand new ones? Is this not the epitome of discrimination against the longsuffering women of Islam? That kind of Islamic heaven makes Hollywood look like a monastery. The exceedingly holy God would have nothing to do with such a whoring place.

It is astonishing to note that sensual excesses, which can send one straight to Hell if unrepented of, are exactly what are promised to our Muslim friends in their paradise. There are Bible warnings against such, if you will heed them:

> "Do you not know that the wicked will not inherit the Kingdom of God? Do not be deceived: Neither the sexually immoral nor idolaters nor adulterers nor male prostitutes nor homosexuals nor slanders nor swindlers will inherit the Kingdom of God" (1 Corinthians 6:9-10, NIV).

> "The acts of the sinful nature are obvious: sexual immorality, impurity and debauchery: . . . I warn you, as I did before, that those who live like this will not inherit the Kingdom of God" (Galatians 5:19, 21 NIV).

The passage of scripture that describes your final state if you fail to repent may be found in Revelation 21:8:

> "But the cowardly, the unbelieving, the vile, the murderers [*including Jihadists*], the sexually immoral, those who practice magic arts, the idolaters and all liars – their place will be in the fiery lake of burning sulphur [*hell*]. This is the second death."

Chapter 19

Muhammad or Jesus for Salvation

Muhammad's daughter, Fatima, was perhaps gripped with the reality of the hereafter when she asked her father what her fate would be on the day of judgement. Listen to the "revelation" handed down to Muhammad to give his daughter:

> "Say: I am no bringer of newfangled doctrine among the apostles, nor do I know what will be done with me or you. I follow but that which is revealed to me by inspiration; I am but a warner open and clear" (Sura 46, Al-Ahqaf, Verse 9).

Can you imagine? Muslims claim Muhammad to be the "seal" and "greatest" of the prophets, yet he wasn't sure of going to heaven himself, nor could he offer that assurance to his own daughter. If that is what he believed, why follow him? A religion that cannot grant assurance of salvation to its own prophet will certainly disappoint its lesser adherents in the last day. This uncertainty has characterized the lives of all professing Muslims down through the ages, and it serves as a prelude to their impending doom. But you need not go the uncertain way of Muhammad and Fatima. There is a way out for you. Jesus Christ had a much better answer when Thomas asked Him a similar question:

> "Lord, we know not whither thou goest; and how can we know the way? Jesus saith unto him, I am the way, the truth, and the life: no man cometh unto the father but by me" (John 14:5,6).

This declaration of Jesus does away with the need for all other religions. If you accept Christ, you are not accepting a religion, but a living Savior. He alone can give you the assurance of your salvation:

> "But this man [Jesus] because he continueth ever, hath an unchangeable priesthood. Wherefore he is able to save them to

the uttermost that come unto God by him, seeing he ever liveth to make intercession for them" (Hebrews 7:24, 25).

Islam and the Hope of Muslims

The Koran makes an incredible but true statement concerning their fate that should make every Muslim break out into a cold sweat. The Koran teaches plainly that both "unbelievers" and Muslims will go to Hell-fire. The Koran declares that Muslims will eventually be rescued, but unbelievers (kafir) will remain there. Sura 19, Maryam, verses 67-68, 71-72:

"But does not man call to mind that we created him before out of nothing? So by thy Lord, without doubt, we shall gather them together, and [*also*] the evil ones [*with them*]; then shall we bring them forth on their knees round about hell;

"Not one of you but will pass over it [*hell*]: this is with thy Lord, a decree which must be accomplished. But we shall save those who guarded against evil, and we shall leave the wrong doers therein, [*humbled*] to their knees."

These statements are so explicit that Islamic scholars cannot explain them away. All they can say is that they all will first enter Hell before being saved according to their works. The number of years they will spend in Hell before help arrives is not specified in the Koran.

I do not have a different interpretation of these Koranic verses than the Islamic scholars do. All I can say to my Muslim friends is that Hell is a place of no return. Once you are in there, you are in forever (Sura 6:128; 11:107 cf.. Mark 9:43; Rev.20:10). Even if it were possible to pluck you out of Hell, the promised Islamic paradise is still a sort of Hell since the thrice holy God will have nothing to do with a city full of wine bibbing, adulterous and whoring people.

That an Islamic paradise would not be sin-free is clear from the "balancing theory" – that those whose good deeds outweigh their sins will enter paradise. It is a false hope. One sin disqualifies you from heaven as in the case of Adam and Eve. It takes complete holiness to enter the real heaven (Revelation 21:27; Hebrews 12:14). Our God is so pure that He cannot tolerate even the smallest sin (if there is such a thing as a small sin, Habakkuk 1:13).

If Allah's words are to be believed, then it is totally impossible for a Muslim to escape Hell-fire. In yet another sura of the Koran, Allah emphatically declares that he has ordained all Muslims and jinns to end up in Hell:

> "If we had so willed, we could certainly have brought every souls its true guidance: but the word from me will come true. I will fill hell with jinns and men all together" (Sura 32:13; cf. again, Sura 19:71).

There is just no way this sura can be twisted to yield a meaning other than that Muslims along with jinns shall be in Hell-fire. The sura is so plain that any counter interpretation is impossible.

If Muhammad's words have any meaning for you, they mean that as long as you are under Allah and in Islam, it is his will to fill Hell with you and jinns. If you remain a Muslim, that will surely come to pass just as Allah has said. So that you may be assured that Allah means business, his intent to jampack you and all other Muslims into Hell-fire is reinforced by Sura 11:118, 119.

But the true Bible God has an entirely different message, and a totally different plan. He is not willing that you should go to Hell, but that you should come to repentance and be saved.

> "The Lord is not willing that any should perish, but that all should come to repentance" (2 Peter 3:9).

> "There is therefore now no condemnation to them which are in Christ Jesus" (Romans 8:1).

From the teaching of Jesus we understand that the Bible God did not prepare Hell for mankind, but for Satan and his rebellious angels (Matthew 25:41). You will only end up there if you join Satan in rebellion against God by rejecting the redemption that is in Christ Jesus.

Though you have belonged to a religion that has killed millions of God's people, torn down His altar, sponsored demons to fight against Him, even if you have personally shed Christian blood, or supported those who have – whatever you may have done – God really loves you, and always has. If you truly want to be forgiven, Jesus is stretching forth His hands of love to receive you; for He also said:

"Come unto me, all ye that labor and are heavy laden [*i.e. burdened with sins and guilt*], and I will give you rest" (Matthew 11:28).

The fact that Jesus prayed for His killers is all the reason you need to believe in Him. He will have mercy on you if you humble yourself and repent. Do not harden your heart by saying you believe in Jesus already. You have not believed until you recognize that Jesus is the Son of God, and accept the truth of His atoning death and resurrection. As a Hell-bound sinner, nothing short of the shed blood of Jesus can save you:

"The blood of Jesus Christ his Son cleanseth us from all sin. If we say that we have no sin, we deceive ourselves, and the truth is not in us. If we confess our sins, he is faithful and just to forgive us *our* sins, and to cleanse us from all unrighteousness" (1 John 1:7-9).

Chapter 20

The Islamic
Version of Hell

"Not one of you but will pass over it" (Sura 19:71).[1]

Yusaf Ali in his footnote no. 2518 offers three plausible interpretations for the above, none of which negates the fact that according to Allah, everyone will sink into Hell. The phrase "Pass over it" has led many Islamic theologians to conclude that there might be a bridge (Sirat) spanning Hell.

The length is supposedly great. Probably some millions of kilometers. What about the width? You can be sure it's as thin as a thread. A kind of fiery obstacle course. We shall see on that day how you will scale through a thread like a sirat. While verse 72 hints of a possible rescue operation from the fire, other suras hold out no such hope, Sura 6:128, 11:105-107, 14:16-17, 32:20, etc. So how certain is an Islamic rescue when the creator of the universe – the God of the Bible - declares that those who go to Hell will stay there forever?

The Koran states that Hell has seven gates (Sura 15:44) with nineteen angels guarding them (Sura 74:30-31). The Islamic Hell is a ghastly rather than a ghostly place. It represents an extension and amplification of all the worst physical horrors imaginable in this life. Since sensuality characterizes Islam, inmates of Hell are assured of a constant though horrible meal of it:

- They will eat to their satisfaction from a tree called *Zaqqum* that springs form the bottom of Hell (Sura 37:62-66).

- Another source of bitter food is the plant *Dhari* which neither nourishes nor satisfies (Sura 88:6-7).

---

[1] Sura 19:70-72 is quoted in full on p. 97

- Occupants of Islamic Hell will not suffer thirst. There will be an abundance of boiling water and other equally unpleasant beverages (Sura 37:67).

Feeding of inmates should not be misconstrued to mean mercy on the part of Allah. The meal may be intended to enable them to have the strength to withstand the terrible agony they will suffer as inmates are:

- dragged into blazing fire immediately (Sura 37:68)
- have their skin roasted and renewed (Sura 4:56)
- made to taste boiling fluid, fluid dark, murky and intensely cold (Sura 38:57)
- served either intensely cold or boiling fluid (Sura 78:21-25)
- made to endure a blast of fire, boiling water, shade of black smokes (Sura 56:4-44)
- weighed down with burning chains and beaten with iron clubs (Sura 14:49-50; 22:19-22)
- clothed with garment of fire (Sura 22:19-22)
- neither to die nor to live (Sura 20:74; 87:13)
- forced into the fire each time they try to get away (Sura 32:20)

Mental anguish intensifies the physical pain. No peace here, only interminable wrangling and mutual recrimination (Sura 40:47-50). Relief in death is denied the damned, even in the face of remorse (Sura 60:25-29). Surat Qaf paints a mind boggling conversation between Hell and Allah. Allah asks, "Hell, are you filled up?" The answer comes back, "Are there any more?" (Sura 50:30).

The perfect hatred of Allah toward Jews and Christians comes to the fore again when inmates are distributed among the seven compartments of Hell. These allocations are an interesting sidelight into the Muslim tendency to demonize their opponents.

- Jahannam (Gehenna) for sinners who failed to repent before death is the commonest (mentioned 77 times in the Koran).
- Laza, the place where Christians will languish (Sura 70:15).
- Hutama, the region where Jews will be tortured (Sura 104:5).
- Sa'ir, the abode of demons
- Jahim, a place where pagans burn (Sura 40:7)
- Saqar, the chamber prepared for Zoroastrians (Sura 74:27)
- Hawiya, dwelling place for hypocrites (Sura 101:9).

Punishment in Islamic Hell is under angelic supervision, but there is a striking exemption – Muhammad's uncle, Abu Lahab, who happened to be a bitter foe gets special treatment. In five verses of the Sura titled "Lahab" (Sura 111), Muhammad (sorry, I mean to say Allah) draws a vengeful scenario: Abu Lahab is to burn in perpetuity. His wretched wife (no angels this time) supplies the fagots to keep the inferno going. The Koran falls just short of creating a special compartment for this unfortunate fellow. Islamic tradition paints a picture of additional Hellish horrors, just in case the foregoing images were not frightening enough.

One Hadith sketches a scientific absurdity: that Allah ordered the fire to burn 1,000 years till it turned red, then another 1,000 years till it turned white, and a further 1,000 years till it turned black, supposedly its present color. When the fire complained that it was being consumed, Allah gave it two natures – molten hot in summer, and freezing cold in winter. But that is not what the God of the Bible says Hell is like. There are many references, here are two:

> Mat 13:49-50 So shall it be at the end of the world: the angels shall come forth, and sever the wicked from among the just, and shall cast them into the furnace of fire: there shall be wailing and gnashing of teeth.

> Rev 14:10-11 The same shall drink of the wine of the wrath of God, which is poured out without mixture into the cup of his indignation; and he shall be tormented with fire and brimstone in the presence of the holy angels, and in the presence of the Lamb: and the smoke of their torment ascendeth up for ever and ever.

Chapter 21

Islam
& Christ's
Second Coming

As is common with Satan – the arch-deceiver – he will always pervert what he cannot outright deny. He has led Muslims to believe that Jesus is coming again to kill the anti-Christ (Dajjal), Islamize the world, marry and die, and then be buried. To show that Muslims really believe this demonic eschatology, they have already dug a grave for Jesus alongside that of Muhammad at Medina. (Those that go to Mecca to run round and kiss a black stone, Ka'aba, can bear witness to it). This stupendous lie came forth from the abyss because Jesus Christ will never die again. That grave at Medina will remain empty throughout eternity. Jesus has completely conquered death. The Bible says:

> "For we know that since Christ was raised from the dead, he cannot die again: death no longer has mastery over Him" (Romans 6:9, NIV).

Jesus used the death process to travel to that realm to destroy Satan, sin and death.

> "The reason the son[1] of God appeared was to destroy the devil's work" (I John 3:8, NIV).

---

[1] Editor's Note: The term "Son of God" is not a Christian invention. Jesus was even questioned by His enemies about being the "Son of God," and it is indeed what He knew Himself to be. The Pharisees in Jesus' day fully understood that Jesus declared His sonship, and attempted to kill Him for it several times. The term "Son of God" does not mean that God took a wife in the normal biological process. The Bible concept of Christ's sonship is that God the Father, in love, sent a part of Himself to Earth , in the form of a man, Jesus Christ, His only begotten Son. God sent Jesus to save us from our sins. (See John 1:1-14; 1Timothy 3:16)

Why not allow Jesus to destroy the devil's works in your life?

> "Since the children have flesh and blood, he too [*Jesus*] shared
> in their humanity so that by his death he might destroy him who
> holds the power of death – that is, the devil" (Hebrews 2:14,
> NIV).

Jesus did not wage a Jihad against innocent souls, but against His
archenemy – Satan. He defeated Satan on the cross of Calvary about
2,000 years ago. Satan is only using Islam to launch a counter attack
against Jesus. It will soon come to naught (Revelation 19:20; 20:7-10; 1
Corinthians 15:24-26) Jesus is not coming again to preach, but to first of
all evacuate his followers (1 Thessalonians 4:16, 17) and then punish in
eternal fire all who rejected His Gospel (2 Thess 1:7-8).

Christ will descend with such supernatural power that His glory alone
will dazzle the devil out of action from a range of several million miles.
(See 2 Thessalonians 2:8, cf.. Acts 9:3). Remember, just a tiny amount of
His glory dazed the great persecutor, Saul, on his way to Damascus (Acts
9:3). Were it not for the mercy of our Lord and that Saul repented of his
sins (Acts 9:17, 18), that story would have ended differently.

If Satan himself cannot stand before the power of Jesus Christ, how
much less can you – a mere man – your flesh can even be destroyed by a
tiny malaria mosquito. From whence cometh your arrogance, you who are
made from dust? (Genesis 3:19). Multitudes are already suffering in Hell.
You can join them, too, if you wish, by turning away from the only Gospel
that can save you:

> "He that despised Moses' law died without mercy under two or
> three witnesses: Of how much sorer punishment, suppose ye,
> shall he be thought worthy, who hath trodden under foot the
> Son of God, and hath counted the blood of the covenant,
> wherewith he was sanctified, an unholy thing, and hath done
> despite unto the Spirit of grace? (Hebrews 10:28-29)

Chapter 22

A Final Word
to Muslim Readers

Contrary to the view held by most Muslims, that Jesus is for the Jews only, Jesus is the promised Messiah (Al-Masih) who will save anyone who calls upon Him in faith. Since God first gave His law to the Israelites, Jesus ordered that the Gospel be preached to them first (Matthew 10:6). God has to start somewhere. Later on, Jesus gave the following command:

"Go ye into all the world, and preach the gospel to every creature. He that believeth and is baptized shall be saved; but he that believeth not shall be damned" (Mark 16:15, 16).

It's high time we stop playing politics with God. He is not interested in our doctrinal gymnastics, nor in any religion that cannot solve the sin problem. You can be as religious as it is possible to be, and still go to Hell. God says you are a sinner (Romans 3:23). Down inside, you know it to be true. Your conscience bears witness that you are. As a sinner, the sentence of eternal death in Hell has been passed on you (Ezekiel 18:14; Romans 6:23). Hiding under the religious umbrella of Islam cannot take away your death sentence. You are depraved and corrupted as a result of sin. Before an absolutely holy God, you are as dirty as a pig, if not more so. Sin, which is totally offensive before God, is not dealt with in Islam. In short, Islam has no answer at all for your sin problem. No wonder it prescribes external washings as a solution (Sura 5:7). Jesus identifies the heart as the source of man's problem:

"for out of the heart proceed evil thoughts, murders, adulteries, fornications, thefts, false witness, blasphemies"(Mat 15:19).

Except you allow Jesus to perform spiritual heart surgery in you, you will not be fit for the Bible heaven. God requires a pure heart (Matthew 5:8) and complete holiness (Hebrews 12:14). But Christ loves you so much that He made special provision for your spiritual heart surgery by shedding His blood on the cross of Calvary. It is His shed blood, and faith in Him alone, that can remove sins from your rotten heart (1 John 1:7). Jesus said,

> "Except a man be born again, he cannot see the Kingdom of God" (John 3:3).

Sin is a spiritual problem requiring a spiritual solution.

It is downright impossible for a sinner to sneak into the real heaven. The exceedingly holy God would not allow it, the angels would kick him out, and heaven itself would spew out such a one. Assuming a sinner were to be admitted into heaven without the new nature, he would soon feel so miserable, and eventually die of his sinful appetites since the true heaven would lack sinful facilities. You must come to Christ to receive the new nature which was purchased for you by His blood (1 Corinthians 15:49) if you desire to go to the real heaven.

You need not waste your money on a pilgrimage to some so-called "holy place," for Christ can meet you right where you are. God is omnipresent. Don't waste money on rams; the blood of rams can't wash away your sins. A single human soul is worth more than all the rams on earth. ONLY THE BLOOD OF JESUS can cleanse you of your sin.

Why not repeat this prayer?

"Lord Jesus, I realize I am a sinner. I know I have been deceiving myself. I now repent of all my sins and false religion. I believe You died for my sins and rose again the third day for my justification. I henceforth accept You as my Lord and personal Savior. Please blot my name out of the book of Hell and write it in the book of Life. Thank You for saving me."

If you recite this prayer from the depths of your heart, and mean it, then you are on your way to heaven, for thus sayeth the Lord God . . .

> Rom 10: 9-10 "That if thou shalt confess with thy mouth the Lord Jesus, and believe in thy heart that God has raised Him form the dead, thou shalt be saved. For with the heart man believeth unto righteousness,; and with the mouth confession is made unto salvation."

Chapter 23

A Final Word
to Christians

This book was not written as a higher criticism of Islam, but so that both Christians and Muslims could have a knowledge of the true nature of Islam. Having now read this book, Christians should see the need for being effective fishers of Muslims through the enabling of the Holy Spirit.

It is sad to note that Christianity has had little impact on the Islamic world. Christ has gotten very few converts from Islam when compared with those from other religions.

I proffer the following five reasons:

(1) Islam, being anti-Christian to the core, prejudices its adherents against the Gospel right from infancy.

(2) We have not really displayed God's kind of love toward them.

(3) Most of us fear Muslims as if they are dynamite.

(4) Unbelief and procrastination on our part – coupled with the apathy of the church toward Muslim evangelism.

(5) We have not taken pains to understand Islam (How many Christians have any idea what the Koran teaches?)

I want to say here, those Christian brethren in Nigeria who think they can flee South for safety when the Muslims strike, need to re-think their position. The reason being: the Muslims still eye the South, since the original plan of the Jihadists was to bury the Koran in the Atlantic Ocean. The solution is evangelism. It is not in fleeing southward, nor to anywhere else, for that matter. Evangelism is God's command and we can't disobey it and expect God's blessing. Muslims will cease to be a threat if we evangelize them, so we do ourselves a favor if we heed God's call.

God could be using the children of Hagar, the "bondwoman,"as His chastening rod for the church (in the same way that He used Nebuchadnezzar against the Israelites).[1] If we really believe the Gospel, we must reject the spirit of Jonah (to flee to Tarshish). We must reach out to Muslims with the Gospel of God's love, for the Bible says:

> "Neither is there salvation in any other: for there is no other name under heaven given among men whereby we must be saved" (Acts 4:12).

Jesus has also paid for their salvation with His own precious blood and He even obtained a receipt as evidenced by His triumphant resurrection. Any Muslim that now dies and goes to Hell is a loss to Christ. And Christians who do not witness will not be innocent on that day (Isaiah 56:10, 11; Ezek. 3:17, 18). Refusing to preach the Gospel is the worst of crimes, with eternal consequences. Let us arise, for the King's business requires haste. Further delay could be disastrous. The results belong to God (1 Corinthians 3:6).

---

[1] Editor's Note: Brother Ali is referring to the Scripture that identifies the children of Hagar (the Arabs) as children of a bondwoman: Gal 4:24-25 "This is allegorically speaking: for these *women* are two covenants, one *proceeding* from Mount Sinai bearing children who are to be slaves; she is Hagar. Now this Hagar is Mount Sinai in Arabia, and corresponds to the present Jerusalem, for she is in slavery with her children." And most Arabs, and much of the third world, are indeed in unwitting slavery to a false religion.

Bibliography

Ali, A. Yusuf, *The Quran: Text, Translation and Commentary*

Badawi, J., *Jesus in the Koran and the Bible*, an outline (Pamphlet) Islamic Foundation, Canada.

Bivando, V & Moucarry, C. *Reaching Muslim For Christ*, International Fellowship of Evangelical Students (1984)

Deedat, A., *Christ in Islam*, Islamic Propagation Center, Durban.

Jeffery, A., *Materials for the History of the Text of the Koran*, New York: AMS Press (1975)

Madany, B. M., *The Bible and Islam*, Back to God Hour, Palos Heights, U.S.A. (1987)

Masih, Abd-Al, *Islam under the Magnifying Glass*, Light of Life Austria.

Miller, M. William, *A Christian Response to Islam*, Presbyterian and Reformed, London (1976)

Pflander, C. G., *The Balance of Truth* (The Mizanu'l Haqq) (enlarged), Light of Life, Villach, Austria (1986)

Pickthall, M. Marmaduke, *The Meaning of the Glorious Koran*, Islamic Publications Bureau, Lagos.

Rafique, *Kinsmen of Abraham*, Grace and Truth Inc. (1989)

Shorrosh, Anis, *Islam Revealed: A Christian Arab View of Islam*, Thomas Nelson & Sons, Nashville, (1980)

Skolfield, E. H., *Hidden Beast 2*, Fish House Publishing, Fort Myers, (1991)

Sumerall, Lester, *Time Bomb in The Middle East*, Harrison House, Tulsa, (1994)

Thomas, R. W., *Islam: Aspect and Prospects*, Light of Life, Villach, Austria.

Tisdal, W. St Clair, *Christian Reply to Muslim Objections*, Light of Life, Villach, Austria (1980)

A Response to
Louis Farrakhan's
Anti-Christian
Propaganda

by Don Richardson
1996

ENSLAVED GIRL IS NO MYTH YET THERE'S SILENCE

Thomas Sowell, Stanford, Calif.

Daily News, Los Angeles, CA, 02/14/97

A haunting picture of a thin and forlorn-looking African girl has this caption under it: "A 12-year old girl, given up as a slave to atone for a crime by a member of her family, stands at the beck and call of a traditional priest in Tefle, Ghana." This is not a painting of something that happened long ago. It is a photograph that appeared in The New York Times of Feb. 2, 1997.

According to local customs, some crimes can only be atoned for by the family's giving up one of its young virgins for sexual enslavement.

I have not seen a word of comment, much less outrage, from any of those who cry out so loudly about slavery in centuries past among people long dead. Not only does slavery persist to this moment in the backwaters of Ghana, it persists on a larger scale in Sudan and in Mauritania, which has about 30,000 people still in bondage, often under brutal conditions.

This is Black History Month, but this part of that history is being swept under the rug. Far more popular are the myths that cater to current psychological and political needs, like the image of Kunta Kinte in "Roots," puzzled by the chains clapped on him – even though slavery was widely known in the part of Africa from which he came, long before the first white man appeared on the scene.

Challenged by professional historians, Alex Haley's reply was: "I tried to give my people a myth to live by." No doubt Haley's intentions were good, but it is the truth that sets you free, not myths.

The most painful of all truths is that slavery existed all over this planet, among people of every race and color, for thousands of years. Nobody wanted to be a slave, but that is completely different from saying that they oppose slavery for others. Slavery was as accepted in Africa as it was in Europe or Asia, or among the indigenous peoples of the eastern Hemisphere.

Incredibly late in human history, a mass moral revulsion finally set in against slavery – first in 18th century England and then, during the 19th century, throughout Western civilization. But only in Western civilization.

ABOUT four years ago CNN's Larry King, on *Larry King Live*, interviewed Louis Farrakhan, head of The Nation of Islam. King asked Farrakhan why he advises Christian Afro-Americans to turn from Christianity to Islam. Farrakhan replied that Christianity is the religion of those who enslaved Africans. Islam, he said, has always championed the black race, and thus deserves the loyalty of Afro-Americans.

Larry King hadn't done his homework. He was unprepared to ask Farrakhan questions which could have made the interview far more lively, not to mention embarrassing for Farrakhan.

Around that time my son Paul took a course in African history at Cal State Fullerton – a course taught by a Muslim professor from Kenya. The professor leveled the same charge: Christianity consistently abetted the enslavement of black Africans; Islam traditionally opposed the heinous practice.

Paul later told me, "As the only Christian in the class, I was embarrassed. I didn't know what to say. Was he right?"

Meanwhile more and more Muslim teachers worldwide are spreading a triumphal claim that a majority of black people in America have already converted to Islam. Descendants of the very people Christians took to America as slaves, they assert, have by Allah's mercy become the means whereby America is at last being drawn to Islam.

The King of Saudi Arabia recently invited Louis Farrakhan to a palace in the heartland of Islam and gave him a sizeable financial reward for his success in converting Afro-Americans to Islam. Flashbulbs popped as Muslim news media prepared to announce Farrakhan's success across the Islamic world.

Indeed, some black pastors in America have grieved to see an occasional young black man leave the church to join Farrakhan. The Nation of Islam continues, meanwhile, to match what Christians have often done by serving black communities across America with inner city development projects. Because of the amounts of Muslim oil money funneled to Farrakhan, the Nation of Islam can often exceed the scale of Christian humanitarian aid. The Nation of Islam also ingratiates itself to black communities by its zealous rehabilitation of black men incarcerated in prisons and by gestures such as paying the legal expenses of the black men who were accused of beating Reginald Denny in the recent Los Angeles riots.

Millions of black people in America have long regarded Abraham Lincoln, a Christian, as a virtual "saint" – a deliverer of the black race. Louis Farrakhan is not pleased to hear a Christian thus commended. In his address carried nationwide by CNN on the occasion of "The Million Man March" in Washington, D. C., Farrakhan sneeringly referred to Abraham Lincoln as "our supposed deliverer."

How should Christians, especially black pastors, respond? They may want to begin by reading The *Encyclopedia Britannica's* piece on the history of slavery. There we learn that "slave" in English derives form the word "Slav." The Romans, in a time when slavery was practiced worldwide, brought captives from Slavic Europe and sold them as slaves in the Roman Empire. Procedures for caravanning safely over the formidable Sahara to bring slaves from distant, unmapped black Africa were still unperfected.

After Islam spread across North Africa in the 600's, Muslim entrepreneurs in the 700's charted routes from oasis to oasis and proved that if large numbers of slaves were brought from below the Sahara, enough would survive to assure a profit.

Slaver caravans from Muslim regions now known as Morocco, Algeria, Tunisia, Libya and Egypt struck out on dire southward journeys. For practical reasons Muslim slavers themselves did not raid for slaves among the northernmost black tribes such as the Hausa and the Fulani. Instead they coerced the Hausa, Fulani and others to be the ones who actually dirtied their hands as slave raiders. Muslims needed only to supply the most northerly black tribes with the chains, manacles and swords they needed to efficiently kidnap people from tribes living further south.

Muslim slave traders paid the northernmost black tribes a wholesale price for those seized. Slaves surviving the long march to North African cities were sold there at retail prices.

Other Muslim slavers from Arabia and Egypt sailed down the East African cost and formed a slave-gathering base on an island called Zanzibar. Equipping mainland black tribes adjacent to Zanzibar as slave raiders, they too saw their profits grow.

Muslim slavers soon brought teachers of the Koran to convert, not just any subSaharan black tribe, but only those that agreed to kidnap and sell their neighbors to the south. Islam thus established itself along the 4,000-mile southern edge of the Sahara form Senegal to Somalia, and among coastal tribes near Zanzibar. Question! Why did Islam not spread much, much further across subSaharan Africa? Alas, this is where the *Encyclopedia Britannica's* otherwise excellent history of slavery falters. It fails to even <u>ask</u>, let alone answer, such an intriguing question.

Understandably, Islamic missionaries brought to subSaharan Africa by Muslim slavers could not convert more southerly African tribes. People harried by Muslim-induced slave raids were far from eager to convert to the religion of the raiders. Muslims who ventured to victimized tribes, even for peaceful purposes, would meet vengeance. Further, Islamic law forbids Muslims to enslave Muslims, hence converting tribes which were the source of slaves would interfere with slave-trading profits.

Christians in Europe thus unwittingly granted Islam a 1000-year head start in altering the destiny of subSaharan Africans. Yet Muslim missionaries, by siding with Muslim slavers instead of opposing them, forfeited the enviable advantage that 1000-year head start afforded. Had they opposed slavery instead of condoning it, Muslim missionaries could have spread Islam all the way from the Sahara to Africa's southern tip. Teaching the Koran, building Mosques and founding Islamic schools with not a hint of contest from Christians, they could have Islamicized an entire continent.

Christian missionaries, arriving belatedly in the early 1800's, would have had to struggle to win even a tiny beachhead *anywhere* in black Africa. Planting churches in Zimbabwe and Zululand would have been as difficult as planting churches in Algeria and Libya.

Muslims in those days little dreamed that a later century would bring scores of woefully late but zealous Christian missionaries from Europe and America to the very tribes Muslim missionaries had consigned as prey for Muslim slavers. Had such a premonition crossed Muslim minds, Islam might have ended its complicity with the slave trade industry. All of black Africa as far as Cape Good Hope would then have been Islamicized with relative ease *centuries* before the first Christian incursion.

Instead, though they arrived ruefully late in black African history, a relative handful of Christian missionaries have caused 250 million black Africans in subSaharan Africa to be categorized today as Christian! Yes, Christian missionaries consistently opposed slavery everywhere they encountered it. In Uganda, David Livingstone often found himself looking into the muskets of Muslim slavers who were incensed at a Christian who urged them to end something they had been doing with impunity for a millennium.

But on the coast of Nigeria, Mary Slessor found herself opposing her fellow-Europeans who were slavers. Let us now turn to the matter of Christian involvement in the slave trade. The *Encyclopedia Britannica* names Roman Catholics from Spain and Portugal as first among Christians to take slaves form black Africa, beginning in the 1600's. Ill-advisedly following the by then 900-year-old bad example of Muslims across North Africa, Spanish and Portugese slavers, not needing to brave the Sahara, sailed around the great bulge of West Africa, seeking slaves. Later some other European nations and eventually the southern American colonies joined the evil practice. The northern colonies and Canada, my own home country, refused to legalize slavery and even gave sanctuary to slaves fleeing from the southern colonies.

An important question must be asked: which group among the actual slave-owning societies first began to manifest twinges of conscience over the horrors of slavery – Christian slave-owning societies or Muslim slave-owning societies?

Slavery was not declared illegal in Saudi Arabia, the main guardian of Islamic purity, until 1965. Nor was slavery declared illegal in Muslim Sudan until 1991. Six years ago, a *Time* cover story entitled "Slavery in the Twentieth Century" documented slavery as a nominally illegal but still common practice across Muslim areas of Saharan Africa. *Reader's Digest*, in its March 1996 issue, published an article entitled "Slavery's Shameful Return to Africa." It focuses on Muslim enslavement of several thousand black Christians in the Southern Sudan. *African Rights*, based at 11 Marshalsea Road, London SE1 1EP England, recently published a book entitled "Facing Genocide: the Nuba of Sudan." Slavery is one of the weapons of that genocide.

Most recently, *The Economist* (9/21/1996) published a piece entitled "The Flourishing Business Of Slavery." I quote:

"The American embassy in Sudan acknowledges as "credible," reports that (Christian) Dinka and Nuba children from southern Sudan are being sold on into Libya. London based *Christian Solidarity International* has ransomed 20 Sudanese slaves. The going rate for a woman is 5 cows.

"The Sudanese government flatly denies that slavery exists there. It is lying. Evidence from human rights organizations, exiles, traders and former slaves is overwhelming. Louis Farrakhan...occasional guest of the Libyan and Sudanese governments, has rebuffed assertions of slavery in Sudan as Zionist claptrap. Last March, he challenged journalists to go to Sudan and find it. Two reporters from the *Baltimore Sun* did just that and published their findings in June, sparking a lively debate among black Americans about how they – and black Muslims in particular – should respond to the plight of enslaved black Africans."

Why do Muslim nations "renounce" slavery nominally and then deny its existence when it persists? Quite obviously they are disinterested in the moral issue. Two persuasions have proved effective: 1. Muslim governments sensitive to international peer pressure from predominantly Christian nations in Europe and the Americas had to "end" slavery, at least on paper, or be viewed as barbarian. 2. Muslim nations indifferent to world opinion still may have a reason given in an item boxed with *The Economist* article quoted above: "To appease western aid donors"!

What caused many Christians, on the other hand, to refuse to own slaves even when other Christians justified their crime? What caused slavery-opposing Christians to take the lead in mounting a determined effort to see all slaves set free?

Successive Christian reform movements in northern Europe, coupled with a series of Christian renewals in America, finally inspired many Christians to apply an already acknowledged but under-taught Biblical idea to the problem of slavery. That was the belief that God created all men in His own image, and thus has endowed them with 'certain inalienable rights' which must be respected as surely as God must be obeyed.

William Wilberforce, James Chamberlain and Abraham Lincoln were three among many aroused Christians who strove tenaciously until slavery was abolished in Great Britain, all British colonies and the southern United States. Their cause was aided by several hundred Christian missionaries. Arriving among that large majority of black Africans who *by design* had been left as non-Muslims, Christian missionaries not only opposed slavery in Africa itself but *also* bombarded public opinion across Europe and America with letters graphically describing the brutality of both Muslim and Christian slave-gathering. The hymn "Amazing Grace" was penned by one slave trader who renounced his former ways as criminal even if "legal." His recounting of slaver cruelty also helped arouse public opinion in Christian countries.

In the United States, southern insistence on condoning slavery and northern determination to abolish it triggered a bloody civil war that killed 600,000 white men and wounded 2 million others. This century's 10-year war in South Vietnam took 56,000 American lives, yet 53,000 Americans died at Gettysburg – in just one three-day Civil War battle!

Some may object that the northern colonies should have insisted on the abolition of slavery at the time of the union in 1776. Had they done so, the southern states would have refused to join the union. They would have formed a separate sovereign state, in which case there would have been no federal government with a legal right to take southern states to task later.

Let us dare to ask a question the *Encyclopedia Britannica* tactfully avoids: In which Muslim nation has there been even a minor civil disturbance of conscience over slavery, let alone a civil war? Not one. Surely some Muslims wealthy enough to own slaves have declined on principle to buy them. Yet there seems no record of any entire community or sect within Islam that has – prior to this century – opposed slavery and actively worked for its abolition.

Yet Farrakhan gives the northern states no credit for their costly stand. He tars all Christians as abettors of slavery while conspiratorially hiding Islam's 900-year head start in the enslavement of black Africans. He ignores North African and Arabian Muslim responsibility for seducing not all, but some Christian nations, into following their vile example.

There is one more point: Nearly 30 million descendants of slaves brought to America live in America today. Yet vastly greater numbers of blacks were taken as slaves to Muslim North Africa and the Middle East over a much longer time. Why do we not find perhaps 100 to 300 million of their descendants living in North Africa and the Middle East today?

Some Blacks across subSaharan Africa remember the reason. It is a reason the *Encyclopedia Britannica* overlooks: Muslim slavers commonly castrated black males lest they pose a sexual threat to Muslim women in North Africa and Arabia. Those who *are* descended from black slaves, like Mauritania's 1 million *Haratin*, tend to be descended from black *female* slaves sexually exploited by Arab masters, not from male and female black slaves.

Muslim slave owners saw no need to breed slaves. The supply was plentiful. Prices were reasonable. So they inhumanely denied their male slaves not only wages and freedom, but even worse, the rights of marriage, sex and parenting.

While *Time, Readers Digest* and *The Economist* have exposed at least the most recent links between Islamic governments and the practice of slavery, another widely read periodical largely fails to balance in its historical reports on slavery. Every few years, *National Geographic* publishes another major article on the Euro-American slave trade. Are the Geographic editors unaware that for every slave taken from black Africa by Christians, at lest twenty were abducted by Muslims? Yet the Islamic slave trade hides unnoticed.

Now, ironically, Muslim teachers across West Africa combine *National Geographic* articles on Christian involvement in slavery with Islamic anti-Christian diatribes. They use Farrakhan's "spin" to turn Africans against Christianity in the very nations where Muslims began to enslave black Africans nine centuries before Christians became involved, and where Christian missionaries help turn the tide against both Muslim and Christian enslavement!

Bear in mind that several generations have passed since the British and other European colonial powers banished both European and Muslim slave-trading from subSaharan nations such as Nigeria, Ghana and Cameroon. Non-Muslim people in such areas remained illiterate prior to European colonial intervention, so they had no written record of their own precolonial history – until Muslim scholars gave them a record with Islamic villainy erased and Christians alone featured as slavers. Lessons taught repeatedly in school soon seem more real than a memory of long-dead great grandad's tales of a curse coming not only by ship from the west, but also by caravan from the north.

In the interest of fairness, the *Encyclopedia Britannica* invited a few Muslim scholars to contribute to its history of slavery. Unable to present facts to improve Islam's bad image in that history, they nevertheless got in one parting shot in the parting paragraph. Acknowledging that Muslims owned slaves, they added a claim that Muslim slave owners rarely forced their slaves to do hard physical labor out-of-doors. Christian slave owners on plantations in the southern states, on the other hand, forced their slaves to "tote that barge and lift that bale" in any kind of weather.

Lack of massive irrigation projects rendered North Africa and Arabia incapable of supporting large cotton plantations in previous centuries. Groves of date palms near oases were probably the largest agricultural enterprises. If vast fields of cotton could have been planted across North Africa and the Middle East, who believes sympathy would have kept Muslim slave owners from sending their chattels outdoors to do the harder kind of labor?

My son Paul, armed with the above insights, returned to Cal State Fullerton the next week. He spoke up in the next African history class taught by the Muslim professor. Very politely he corrected the one-sided view of the history of slavery the professor had given. Cornered and awed, the professor acknowledged Islam's long precedent in the history of slavery. Then he repeated the same closing comment that the Muslim contributors had added in the *Britannica's* closing paragraph: Muslims did not force their slaves to perform hard outdoor labor. Instead they assigned only menial household tasks to them. Paul was ready with an answer on that as well!

In summary, Christianity's record regarding black African human rights, in spite of horrifying chapters, still far outshines Islam's record on the same. Let Africans, Afro-Americans and Christians everywhere give answer to Mr. Farrakhan's propaganda.

Islam has no hymn like "Amazing Grace," but we do. Let us sing it reverently, as a deeply-felt testimony from our hearts. Let us rejoice because that amazing grace enabled many who follow Jesus to alleviate the suffering of millions who perhaps would still be slaves today, had not that grace moved within our ranks.

FINIS